REVERSE
THE
TIDE

GOD CAN TURN IT AROUND
IN
JESUS CHRIST

REVERSE
THE
TIDE

GOD CAN TURN IT AROUND
IN
JESUS CHRIST

JOSEPH HARRIS

Destiny House Publishing, LLC

REVERSE THE TIDE

Published by Destiny House Publishing, LLC

Copyright © December 2013 Joseph Harris

International Standard Book Number:

ISBN-13: **978-1936867400**

Unless otherwise stated, all scripture quotations are from the Holy Bible, King James Version. Scripture references that do not have the Bible version noted are the author's paraphrase.

Original printing 2013

Cover design. Editing and Publication Layout:

Destiny House Publishing, LLC.

Printed in the United States of America

For information:

Destiny House Publishing, LLC

www.destinyhousepublishing.com

P.O. Box 19774 - Detroit, MI 48219 - 888.890.4555

REVERSE THE TIDE

Table of Contents

INTRODUCTION

The purpose for this book is to reveal and enlighten us of God's reversing power of things that happen in our lives that only he can change. He also helps us understand by faith in God; people can make choices that lead to reversing that old lifestyle to a lifestyle of holiness and goodness as you follow Jesus Christ. Make the right decision today so that God can reverse the tides in your life. I pray that God's word highlights the application of God's principles and blessings for you. Most of us know the destruction hurricanes and floods can cause in our lives. We want God to reverse those kinds of tides in the life of those that have not accepted Jesus as well as those who are saved. The enemy will send legions in the world to tamper with your life. You need Jesus. This scripture will help you see well as you explore the gravity and significance of His word. We pray it will shape your life and move you to another level as a servant and witness testifying among other people that Jesus is Lord and he will anchor you so that those tides of life will not take you and drown you and your precious family.

Take a moment and thank God for blessings that He alone has given us already, and the future plans mapped out for our lives. Thank Him for His mighty wonders and tender mercies. Thank Him for being Sovereign, Omnipotent and Omnipresent and the only true and wise God. Thank Him for being our Supreme Ruler and the Head of our lives and the Church. Thank Him for allowing us to acknowledge His Holy name Jesus Christ, Son of the living God, which is glorious with all power and authority. Thank Him that He allows us to glorify Him alone. Thank Him that He is divine. Thank Him that he builds our character to be like His. We are thankful that He is infallible. He has neither spot nor wrinkle. He is perfect in every way. He is the only wise and true God. Thank Him for all things. I started writing this book because I personally get blown away in the Spirit of how good God has been in my life and how He continues to bless us over and over again.

God wants people everywhere to know that He is able to turn

situations around. He can do it by His power because He is God. The book is written so that everyone will seek God not only in troubled times, however, seek Him because of your relationship and because you need to worship God in spirit and in truth. The word of God in this book is directing you to the Bible where God is speaking to your heart to a greater degree. The word of God is sharper than a two-edged sword. It can penetrate everything you are made of and your circumstances. The Lord our God wants us to know that He can turn it around. You must have hope and believe in the power of Jesus Christ and His will for your life. Ask God to reverse the tide in your life. Ask God to turn things around that are blocking your blessings and hindering you. When things are going in the wrong direction in life, ask God to reverse those destructive things, those barriers.

CHAPTER 1

BLESSED IN GOD'S CREATION

Genesis 1:1-31

GENESIS 1:1 In the beginning God created the Heavens and the Earth.

God was always present. He controls the beginning of time. Without Him, there could be no beginning. God created all things and blessed them for His Purpose. God is good and harbors no evil acts. God can stop war anytime He desires. There is nothing too neither hard nor impossible for God. . However, He allows man to make a choice between good or evil. He desires that man be obedient and make the right choices in life to please Him. God already knows which side man will take. He already knows the level of destruction that man and rulers of every country harbors in their hearts and minds. God can reverse the tides of war in order that lives could be spared, changed and saved (born again) for the purpose of the Kingdom. However, man has an obligation to make a choice. Jesus Christ is waiting for people to acknowledge him and his creative power so He can reverse the tide in their lives whether it is personal living or professional. He can turn things around for you today. You need to submit to Jesus Christ as Lord of your life now.

President Barack Obama's inauguration was 20 January 2009 as the first African American President. His inauguration was largest event in Washington D.C in the history of this nation. Soon after, decisions were made and progress was in the making to start sending troops home from Iraq and some from Afghanistan. The invasion of Iraq war started 20 March 2003. This is a sign of reversing the tide of war and battles to return sons and daughters home. President Obama would also sign into law within his first two years an economic stimulus package. It is time to get peace. Once Soldiers get home and start the healing process, our prayer is that Soldiers get into the house of God and go before the alter and accept Jesus as Lord and Savor. Reversing the tide happens in healing and acceptance of the living Savior. The power of the Holy Spirit can help you turn it around. Whatever it is, the Holy Spirit will turn it around. You need to accept Jesus as Lord. Things change in your life when have Jesus in your life. It is because you have been bowing down to the wrong God. You surrender and bow to the only King of glory, Jesus Christ.

War involves for the most part combat which means someone will engage to kill or destroy the other person in combat. Certainly you are free game to them as well. The enemy is after you on every front, starting with your soul and then your family's souls. You need to reverse the tide and fight back for your family. You need to help them survive in the wicked world. God created the power of love over war so that people could come to Jesus Christ rather than run from war. During world wars, history was being made. It was being made in so many facets of life and certainly on the battlefield. Certainly because of these wars, crises were at its highest, challenges are given and new ideas are birthed. In this case, since the war had been a war of surprise attack on the United States at Pearl Harbor, it erupted something in man and awakened a sleeping giant which was stated by the President of the United States of America. Japan had started something and all hell was about to break loose on the Republic of Japan. During that time, production was at its highest demand for fighting machines. The need was simply weapon systems and men capable of fighting on the battlefield, land, air and ground troops. It was perhaps the same in WWI. Hitler with his invasion all across the world was attacking multiple countries in a quest to control the world. He wanted world supremacy. War leaders strive to win and take control of the world. The United States of America maintains the status of the leader of the world. Peace and tranquility must be at the forefront of leaders in government and all over the world. The United States had to develop in masses new Tanks such as Bradley and Abrams fighting machines, Stealth fighters, F15, 16,17s Jets and bombers to take control of the situation that had gotten out of hand. They had to train men on the ground and in the air. Life had changed. The point is that it takes creativity in designing all the fighting machines that it would take to defeat the enemy and bring about peace treaties and a safe secure, democratic way of life. In these wars, the soldier was invented. The soldier man who was made by God had to be reinvented to serve the need of Presidents and Generals and the country. It takes a certain level of obedience, craftiness and ingenuity to design, develop and produce this hardware and newly invented man called soldier. So because one man spoke and congress approved, the process had begun. Creation of the new bombers and aircrafts and the fighting soldier had been launched. Creation is God's will and blessing for all mankind. We must understand that He spoke for the good of man and for the progressive blessings to continue to shine and shower our lives all together on this blessed planet called Earth and home.

GOD BLESSED CREATION

We need to understand that God gave us the ability to speak things into the life of others because we are the children of God. We walk in His blessedness. God grants us specific request if we believe and have faith in Him. He can do for anyone according to His will and purpose. We have the power in our tongues. The scripture says, "Death and life is in the power of the tongue." More importantly, we have the power of the resurrection from our Lord, King and Savoir in our hearts and minds. He alone is Supreme, Divine and holy with all power in His hand. God created all things by His own power. He ordained His creation because He is God and He loves what He alone did and can do anytime. I believe blessings were predestined for us before creation was even spoken into existence under His voice.

The meaning of blessing is simple. Blessing means a favor upon your life that you did not receive because of you. It really is similar to grace. Blessing means giving of oneself to another so that person will benefit in life and in multiple ways to bring credit upon God. To be blessed means to prosper in life. It means simple to have favor in your life. We have favor in His grace and we have favor in His blessings. Blessings come because of His grace on our lives. Blessings come in the form of His provision for our lives. We can never believe that we blessed ourselves. Even when we take care of ourselves, it is still the blessing of God that allows us to have strength and the right mind to do so.

Because God is the author and He alone creates blessings, there is an abundant flow of every element in substance and whatever you or I are in need of to be sustained and live the blessed life. God will supply your need. God can never run out of blessings. He can never run out of supply. God never runs out of the desires of your heart. That is why He wants everyone to be a blessing to the poor, needy, and the widows. Whatever the source you desire for your ministry in Christ Jesus or just special need, He is able to deliver. Our minds try to comprehend the amount of unlimited resources that God supplies for His people, but if we realize that God is always blessing us, the spirit of doubt will be removed in your heart and mind. You and I must always trust in the living God. He knows how to give us and fulfill our purpose. He is pleased with His marvelous blessings because the glory must be given to Him in all things. He is the God of abundant blessings.

YOU CAN'T REVERSE GOD'S MOVE

One thing for sure nothing could stop the move of God once he started creating the universe. Nothing can ever stop Him because He is sovereign and supreme with all power. This is just what we want others to see when it comes to God's power. When he reverses the move of the enemy in your life, you begin to walk like you have faith. When He started creating His creation and creatures, He knew exactly what He was doing. I am inspired by my Father in Heaven because He sent His Jesus to die for me. I'm also filled with faith and love in my heart for Him because of what I see Him doing in my life each day. I can testify that He moved in my heart to allow me to come into Salvation and the ministry of Christ. He is the inspiration behind all of my life and all life's lessons and blessings. This particular topic came to mind because of challenges in the church. When you feel rejected and see that things are doctrinally disproportionate, you feel the need to pray and encourage. As long as I trust in God and know that He is the center of my life, nothing can separate me nor stop Him from moving in my life. Men can not move my life. They can affect in some ways, but ultimately, I end up in the hands of the Lord. Things to move: hate and sin.

God started in the beginning by providing a garden for Adam that symbolically represented and replicated paradise for him. We know heaven is a perfect place to live and dwell with our Lord. Jesus said, in my house are many mansions; I go to prepare a place for you. And where I go, you will go. When I was a young man I use to hear those words from my mother that across town they had mansions that were so beautiful. I was wondering why she spoke of those things. She wanted us to have the finer things in life. She knew that you had to work for things you wanted. But she also knew that blessings come from God. You can look in momma's eyes and you could tell she was saying just trust Him and He will not let you down. Momma always made the home just right for us. She never let us down. She was my momma that blessed my heart. If anything, I let her down. That is something that we can't afford to do. We need our mothers and each other more than we can imagine. She made us feel like we lived in the perfect garden. She kept the house just that clean. She manicured the yard and put trees and plants all around the place. When I think about it now I think about how good God really is to provide a mother that loved me so much. I think about how good God is when I remembered that He helped my father to allow me to grow up and become a man. He allowed me to grow up and become responsible. He gave me the room to learn and grow and make my mistakes. He allowed me to grow into manhood. He was my Father and in my heart he will always be number one because of His love for me and his family. Fathers know their seed and know that they need to be blessed. It is built inside them. I know that no one could design us like that but God.

God blessed me with another day to be able to publicly thank Him for all of those blessings from my natural father, blessings only that the Lord could provide through him. At least it was significant enough to make me understand to a certain degree, spiritual life. Now when I view God's blessings, it takes on a new meaning in life. Now I am in awe and amazement of how God made man to love.

GOD MOLDED AND SHAPED!

ISAIAH 64:8 But now, O LORD, thou art our father; we are the clay, and thou our potter; and we all are the work of thy hand.

God is the potter and we are the clay. Only He can put love into a clay pot. It is sheer amazement to think of how God can make a man from the ground and breathe the breath of life into him and bless him all at the same time. He has all the specific designs for us. He is the holder of the blueprints of all His creation including man in His mind. God is so loving He continues to shape and mold us daily to serve His purpose and glorify Him alone.

BLESS THE LORD O' MY SOUL

PSALM 103: Bless the Lord, O my soul; And all that is within me, bless His holy name! Bless the Lord, O my soul, And forget not all His benefits: Who forgives all your iniquities, Who heals all your diseases, Who redeems your life from destruction, Who crowns you with loving kindness and tender mercies, Who satisfies your mouth with good things, So that your youth is renewed like the eagle's.

BENEFITS OF BLESSINGS

God revealed and provide benefits of blessings that we must grab hold of them.. David was focused on the good things that God had done for him. He was not complaining about the tough times. Surely he would discover those time in his life. Too many complaints can easily enter your mind and your spirit man then cause you to fumble and use excuses to stop your worship and service. Next thing you know everyone is calling you a complainer. It is better to have praise on your mind at all times than to have worldly praise. When David thought about the benefits in God's blessings he praised Him. He praised God for His power of forgiveness.

David praised God for His healing power. He had seen God's hand heal people. He had seen God's hand healing himself and his family. He could never forget the wrong that God healed his heart when he

18

robbed Uriah of his wife by sending him on the front line of war. When David thought about the healing power it takes to get you from that condition to being healed in the Lord, it makes you want to praise Him. You may have had a similar problem in life. You thought you could never heal until you met God. All anyone needs to do is call on Him and He will answer.

He focused on the fact that God redeems our lives from destruction. You can be walking on the wrong path of life and find yourself at the lowest point of life. You can look around and see that all the time you had walked with the wrong crowd. You could have been dealt a blow in life and it appears no one cares about you. Some tragedy could have shaken your faith and you walked away from God because you question Him about that situation. Why God? Why did you not save my family member? Why did you leave me? Why did I not get rich and my friends did? Those are a lot of whys. Please remember this: God said, "I will never leave you nor forsake you." In the midst of all those whys to God, also ask yourself, why have I not chosen you Father in heaven? This is good time to fill the void in your life. Do not let death and sin push you away from Him at all.

The bible tells us in Jeremiah also that God has a plan for our lives. So, do not ever think it is over because of tragedy or other circumstances. We do not know the full plan. Just like we do not know when tragedy or circumstances that hurt will arise. We don't know when God will open the windows of blessing at one time on you. We do know that He is blessing us right this moment. In fact, there are some things He uses to allow us to get a close relationship with Him so He can bless us abundantly. You may not know right now, but it will be revealed to you. Job experienced perhaps one of the most tragic situations in the Bible. He was broken, broken! He had lost almost His entire family, with the exception of his wife. He lost them because He was a faithful, just and upright man before God. Because he trusted God through the storm, he was blessed with more than he had with the previous family. Even though the enemy wanted him dead, God kept him from the devils grip. It is important to know that when God speaks it is done. He will not let you down, just trust Him. We do not always know what God is up to in our lives. One thing for sure is that we know He is God and has all power in His hand. We do know that He is up to blessing us tremendously. We do know that He loves us so with an everlasting love. David said that He crowns us with His love and compassion. Everyone needs that kind of love. He crowns us as though we are one of His children and walking in holiness. We are heirs of the living King and Savior. He also spoke about satisfying our desires. The scripture says if you delight yourself in the Lord He will give you the desires of your heart(Psalm 37:4).

God loves those who love Him back. The point here is that if you have the talent to express movies, use it for the kingdom of God. Make movies that will be sketch images in your mind and the heart of man. God can use any process that He wants to reveal. In His creation, He reminds us that He is a good of fruitfulness. He spoke in Genesis the command of being fruitful and multiplies.

King David said forget not all my benefits. God benefits us in every moment of our lives. He just does it so openly. Everyone can see it including the angels and those in the lowest cracks of the earth can see He benefits. You see the first benefit of His blessing is life everlasting and the fact that you live now.

HE OWNS CATTLE ON THOUSANDS HILLS

PSALM 50:10 For every beast of the forest is mine, and the cattle upon a thousand hills.

Do you know what it means to have ownership? Everyone wants to own something in life. Whether it is a new car, home, new clothing or even a new business God is the owner. Ownership means to so many a sense of worth and value and success and accomplishment. God owns all things that are created. He owns everything we see or engage in. God made it and ordained exactly what He wanted to create. Man has no say so in what God did. He is God alone and makes His own decisions on what is what. For my life and your life, He stepped right in and blessed us with the abundance of life. Since we know that He owns cattle on a thousand hills, then we know that He can bless us with those cattle and even more according to His purpose for our lives. God is not limited by anything. He made everything. He made oil that men pump out of the ground into well and barrels daily worth billions. He made all the business of the earth that operates under His blessing. Don't be open to anything; God is not pleased with crooked business and crooked places. He operates in truth, so if it is not of God then it is of Satan. God makes crooked places straight for His purpose. God wants us to ask for things according to Matthew, "Ask and it shall be given" "Seek and you shall find" knock and the doors will be open. However, He made it perfectly clear, "We ask God for things but do we really mean it from the heart. The scripture in James 4 and 5 says we ask amiss. We should not ask Him for anything with a wrong motive or wrong heart. We need to be honest with God about all things. He already knows everything. He does not need a lie detector to determine truth or lies. He already knows. Remember the point is that you can own more than cattle on a thousand hills if you trust Him to lead your life in every way. Surrender today to Jesus. He has blessings stored up for you. Get your blessing now.

DOMINION

GENESIS 1:22-28 God blessed them, saying, Be fruitful and multiply, and fill the waters in the seas, and let fowl multiply in the earth. And the evening and the morning were the fifth day. And God said, Let the earth bring forth the living creatures after his kind, cattle, and creeping things, and beast of the earth after his kind, and cattle after their kind, and everything that creeps upon the earth after his kind and: God saw that it was good. And God said, Let us make man in our image, after our likeness: and let them have dominion over the fish of the sea, and over the fowl of the air, and over the cattle, and over all the earth, and over every creeping thing that creeps upon the earth. So God created man in his own image, in the image of God created he him; male and female created he them. And God blessed them, and God said unto them, Be fruitful, and multiply, and replenish the earth, and subdue it: and have dominion over the fish of the sea, and over the fowl of the air, and over every living thing that moves upon the earth.

BE FRUITFUL AND MULTIPLY

God gave dominion to Adam. God gave Adam the authority over everything He created. God blessed Adam and told Him to be fruitful and multiply. It is similar to God telling Abraham and Noah. He wanted these men to bless the earth. He keeps on blessing us even after He created us because we were made for His purpose. He has so many blessings in store for us. God loved Adam so much that He created beast of the field and creeping things on earth and gave Adam full authority over everything. God blessed Adam so much that the Trinity agreed to bless Adam with the power and authority to be in His image. And this power would be beyond measure. No one else on earth had this power but Adam. Adam's entire mission on earth was to reflect God in every way especially in obedience and image. He was not to be God but express himself and carry himself as a man of God. God blessed him that way. He was made to be humble and obedient in the sight of God. God our Lord is so amazing how he alone orchestrated creation. God, our Lord desires for all people to recognize what He has done on this earth and in creation. It would be amazing if God had duplicates of us inside other planets he created. I believe that God wants us to walk in a state of reflecting Him and being appreciative of His amazing blessings in our lives. The Lord our God blessed Adam with a wife. Adam was so satisfied to see that God made a woman and presented him with a beautiful creature called woman.

GOD'S COUNSEL TO MAN

Psalm 1: Blessed is the man who walks not in the counsel of the ungodly, nor stands in the path of sinners, nor sits in the seat of scornful; but his delight is in the law of the Lord, And in His law he meditates day and night. He shall be like a tree Planted by the rivers of water, that brings forth its fruit in its season, whose leaf also shall not wither; and whatsoever he does shall prosper.

Everyone needs counsel. King David received counsel constantly from the Prophet Nathan. Counseling and advising is necessary in all walks of life, all aspects and professions. God is the best to give sound solid counsel because He knows exactly how to touch the mind in its need to be counseled. God gives us psychologist and social workers, case managers and those that deal with psychological affects.

What David stated in this Psalm is extremely powerful. David speaks of man who must be cautious of the company he keeps. The company you keep may give you the counsel that they think is correct. You need God's counsel. He points out that this kind of man is blessed and meditates day and night in the Lord. That is exactly how you get closer to God almighty and have a better relationship. Think of the times you can take just meditating on his word and speaking to Him. Most of us have different ways to meditate. The idea is to let God do what God wants to do through you. David says, man meditate on the law. Law was at one time the school master according to the book of Romans. We know it because even today there are many people confused about grace over the law. But grace came by Jesus Christ and the law by Moses according to the scripture. God gave the law to Moses in the Old Testament in Exodus. The ideas behind the law were to know what God requires of man in living holy and righteous in His sight. The Law was needed because of the nature of man being out of order. His sin was a focus because God always wanted His men to be in His image, not sins image. The scriptures say, in the beginning God created man in His image. Sin was a big problem. So God had to express Himself about it. One example is Sodom and Gomorrah, a place filled with much horrific sin. God rained down brimstone and fire to destroy the entire city. God hates sin that much. He can take the entire world if He wanted to, He made it. The Lord, our God already knows man's ability under the law and under grace. He already knew man would fall in the garden and even after the Garden of Eden experience. That is why grace came by Jesus Christ, the son of God. It would take a blood sacrifice to restore and protect man from his own destruction. No wonder the Psalmist says blessed is the man who walks not in the counsel of the ungodly. If you walk with anything thing outside of godliness you might as well understand and get ready to war against enemy attacks. You see, the bible says that we will judge angels. If you walk avoid those things and walk with Jesus under His perfect counsel, then you will receive the blessings.

MARRIAGE CREATED BY GOD

GENESIS 2:21-24 And the LORD God caused a deep sleep to fall upon Adam, and he slept: and he took one of his ribs, and closed up the flesh instead thereof; And the rib, which the LORD God had taken from man, made he a woman, and brought her unto the man. And Adam said, This is now bone of my bones, and flesh of my flesh: she shall be called Woman, because she was taken out of Man. Therefore shall a man leave his father and his mother, and shall cleave unto his wife: and they shall be one flesh.

The same God who created all things created the institution of marriage. Danny and Shelia Jackson is a prime couple chosen to show how relationships are tested. "Good morning honey, I'm leaving," Danny said to Shelia early on the morning of Oct 17, 2004 as he headed out the door to go to work. Danny notices a sticker on the wall above the bed in Neal's room. Danny exploded at Neal his young son who has been spending time with a group of so called friends who have different belief and values and live by the code to hurt others for no reason. "Danny do your friends have a different social life? What do they do for past time since you are with them?" "I am not with them most of the time" Danny replied. "Have you ever spoken about God to them? I want to remind you that sometimes it just takes one seed of faith to touch somebody else." Danny explained that one of the key elements and circumstances within couples are they always wonder about their true identity. People always want to know where they came from and who they belong to. The identity crisis is here to stay as long as people do not know Him.

CHAPTER 2

GOD'S BLESSINGS ON NOAH!

Genesis 9:1

GENESIS 9: 1-3 And God blessed Noah and his sons, and said unto them, Be fruitful, and multiply, and replenish the earth.

REVERSE THE TIDE: LISTEN AND BE OBEDIENT TO THE VOICE OF GOD AND RECEIVE YOUR BLESSINGS. BE STRONG ENOUGH TO TRAMPLE OVER PLOTS OF EVIL AGAINST YOU WITH THE LOVE OF JESUS CHRIST. BE FRUITFUL AND MULTIPLY BECAUSE GOD CHOSE AND COMMANDED YOU TO DO SO.

RULE YOUR HOUSE OVER THE ENEMY'S PLOT

Jesus conquered the grave and death through His Father's power. He defeated the enemy once and for all by the authority and power of His Father. Then at the end He will dispose of Satan in the pit of brimstone and fire. It is vitally important that we understand that there is constantly a plot against His anointed priest. The enemy plots every moment of the day against God and His priest. No wonder sometimes we feel as though we are up against hell. Priests already know and are protected by the power of God. They actually wear the whole armor of God which must be worn at all times. God priest wear robes of righteousness. With the human eye many may not see it, but God sees the robe that He alone places on His blessed priest. For the man, Priest are God's agents, ambassadors who walk in holiness at all times representing God on earth. They are not gods in any form or fashion. God's priests are men of the household of faith and men who run their homes, keeping it in order. God's priests are men of God that have truly trusted in God in all things. You can't put this priesthood on one day then take it off the next day like we would remove our garments. But you must wear this appointed Priesthood of righteousness for this lifetime and the one to come. Family is at the center of God's will. It started in creation with the first family and that means that God meant for it to be successful and the first ministry that you set out to work on and in. If your house is not in order, why go out and put on a façade, knowing that it is difficult to smile and hug your own family. You must seek God, ask him and believe that he will make you a priest.

God blessed Noah because of his obedience. Noah is viewed as a Priest of his family. He was the perfect model in God's eye. God found grace (favor) in Noah. It was because Noah was obedient and listened to the voice of God and because he was a doer of God's voice and His words. Please understand that Noah had faith in God and his intructions. The enemy was still plotting against Noah but Noah ignored those demons . You need to do the same, ignore the enemy when he is trying to persuade you into sin, doing evil, and of course make you miss church, worship time and your blessing. The blessing on Noah's life could not be reversed because God had favor on Noah's life and his family. You should ignore the devil and walk in obedience. It was the people who did not believe Noah, nor in God voice. Their action did not persuade Noah at all. Noah was obedient in the things of God, not the things of man. I am so joyful that God blessed Noah. Then in return out of his obedience Noah blessed his family. Noah family was blessed because he listened to the voice of God telling him to build the rk that would be responsible for replenish the earth Because Noah heard the Lord speaking to him and he trusted God and acted upon his voice, he and his family was highly blessed by God. His actions continue to bless us today because he put forth the effort and constructed this huge Ark like God told him to do. In our lives we can recall blessings and favor that God granted us when we listened in obedience to him and hearken to His voice. We can hear God's voice like Noah if we dedicate ourselves to Him and get a closer relationship. He blessed Noah to restart the process of multiplying and being fruitful on earth all over again because of His love for mankind. He blessed Noah because he listened close to His voice daily. God wants us to listen to His voice daily and seek Him out for our daily instruction. It is amazing what impact instruction from God can do and how it affected the entire world. He can affect our families and our individual lives in the same manner if we hearken to His voice. I like when Jesus said, my sheep know my voice and follow me. What a blessing! Because He also states that no one can pluck them out of my Father's hand. And it is because of the relationship in the voice and obedience to the Lord. What a blessing to know that my father will not let anything take me out of His hand. So I will listen daily to my Lord.

It appears that Noah can see that family is the backbone in our life. He put God first. He heard the voice of God and took Him seriously. At the same time he managed to guide his family. So the family had to be good listeners as well. We need to understand that there is power in listening and obeying the voice of God. There are times in our lives that problems will occur and more challenges will occur. This could have been seen also as a tremendous challenge to get your family to obey you in the midst of the biggest flood storm that would impact your life.

GENESIS 12:17

PROPHESY WITH MOUNTAIN MOVING POWER

JOEL 2: 28-29 And it shall come to pass afterward that I will pour out My Spirit on all flesh; Your sons and your daughters shall prophesy, Your old men shall dream dreams, Your young men shall see visions. And also on my menservants and on my maidservants I will pour out My Spirit in those days.

I knew you felt that way with all the things you tried to help the family overcome. I promise you I really do. I want you to know that the Lord is going to bless you tremendously. He is going to bless this family because of our Father Joe Arthur Doyle, the man of the house and of course also my mother, Gussie Vance Doyle. They planted seed more than this family can ever imagine. I keep praying that this family will understand the power and the move of God in this family.

My prayer also is that each person in my family will know him as Lord and Savior. We need to keep on trusting or Lord and don't let anything take you away from family. Family is the center and core of God's love. Lord, my prayer is that you pour out your spirit with power that will convert and witness through your people. Pour out your spirit on families. Lord reverses the tide, turn things around in the lives of your people. Thank you father! I hid your word in my heart that I might not sin against you. Whatever you do keep Proverbs 3:5-6 in your heart, in your mind and strength.

RULE YOUR HOUSE AS PRIEST

Jack wanted to be the priest in His house after he heard Barry Smith's wife and children brag on how nice their father is around the house and how he gives so much in support of each one them. They bragged and bragged about Barry to the point that he felt shy and embarrassed. Look at my marriage he said, I am still trying to sort out things. Regina's marriage has experienced some ups and bumps and bruises for 20 years but they hung in there, they keep it working. Somewhere along the time an affair almost happened. It was an innocent kiss but nothing happened.

Jack struggles with that fact because his love for Regina is more than she knows. Jack is now listening to her daughter experiencing boy problems in school. Nichole had a hard crush on a young boy named Daniel. Meanwhile back at home, Jack and Regina were discussing the need to have everyone in the house baptized. They were not the most religious people nor had the full knowledge and authority of what baptism means. But they knew from growing up that it was important. After all, as Jack said, my mother took all of us and made sure we got baptized. It was just something I never forgot because it seemed, at that that time as a little boy, so solemn till it is etched in my mind and has been for the last 42 years. Regina with a very moving look on her face thought it was a good idea.

Regina left and went to the other room and got on her knees and prayed because she was moved with what her husband said and her heart was longing for a true connection. She wanted to know that God was pleased with her. Enough had already gone on at work with the failed financial merger in which she was blamed by Janet her co-worker. Now, she is on the verge of losing her job that she did not realize was being discussed behind closed doors. She needs her job to pay all of her bills. She has a 401K for the kid's college that she needs to keep. Keith is only 12 years, Nichole is 15. College is around the corner. The time will be here before you know it. Jack says to be faithful and allow that weight to go onto the Lord.

Regina pulled over to the side of a highway in tremendous fear of what just took place at work in the conference. She was shaking all over like her nerves were extremely bad. She began telling herself to be cool and calm down. Just a few minutes prior Regina had been in a dispute with a co-worker arguing viciously over a financial project that was suppose to be completed and a deal that was supposed to be closed. The deal was not closed and Janet claimed that it was Regina's fault. Janet needs to make out a report and forward it the CEO, George Ruin. They did not discuss particular reasons for this unfortunate finance breaker. It was clear to Regina in her mind that Janet and George were a click. She also believed that Janet was clicking with every other woman in that business office. To her surprise, she would discover that Janet also was in her personal life. Janet knew her husband as well. (I will save that one for later). Meanwhile the issue at hand was Regina's growing attitude of jealousy.

CHAPTER 3

THE POWER OF YOUR MIND

Philippians 2

GOD WANTS OUR MIND TO REVERSE FROM EVIL TO A GODLY MINDSET BECAUSE GOD'S POWER RESIDES IN OUR MINDS. THERE IS POWER IN YOUR MIND BECAUSE GOD MADE YOU.

REVERSE THE TIDE: The power in your mind can reverse things that are holding you down mentally and in anyway. It is the mind of Christ that will help your through circumstances in your life.

Keep your mind on Jesus Christ and things in Heaven(Colossians 3). Reverse your thought life. Ask God to help stop old thinking and think positive in Jesus Christ. For those who do not know him, it is time to reverse your thoughts and mind set. It is a mind controlled under the anointing of Jesus Christ. It is stable and obedient in Christ. It is a mind that witnesses to the world of His saving grace and mercy. It reminds us that we are anchored in His grace and mercy, and purpose. The anchored mind in Christ is an immovable mind. It is always abounding in the things that please God. This mind is a steadfast mind and immovable He must be the center of your mind. Therefore the Holy Spirit is the only one who can anchor you mind. People cannot anchor your mind. You mind does not need to stay on a person, it must stay on God. That is exactly why we need the Holy Spirit's help and guidance. The Holy Spirit keeps you from being brain washed and over taken by the adversary and his host of demons.

A TRANSFORMED MIND

We are reminded *in Romans 12:1-3 I beseech you therefore, brethren, by the mercies of God, that ye present your bodies a living sacrifice, holy, acceptable unto God, which is your reasonable service. "And be not conformed to this world: but be ye transformed by the renewing of your mind, that ye may prove what is that good, and acceptable, and perfect, will of God"* Romans 12. For I say, through the grace given unto me, to every man that is among you, not to think of himself more highly than he ought to think; but to think soberly, according as God hath dealt to every man the measure of faith. The Apostle Paul urges people to give themselves to God as a sacrifice. He uses the word mercies to express that God will accept you and that this is a holy matter. Jesus wants us to take on the mind of Christ as we allow His spirit to penetrate our mind. He wants us to become synchronized with Him in spirit and thought. It is to our best interest to have a transformed mind and spirit. There are major blessings and benefits in having a relationship. A transformed mind will take you to a new dimension in life. It will first take you into your relation with Jesus Christ. A transformed mind moves you to new levels and helps you to get results.

POWER OF CREATION

God our Father started His initial blessings when He spoke a word and called things to be. In Genesis 1:3, God said, Let there be light, and there was light. There is not any other form of creative power like His. No one else can do it. Look at all the other wanted to be gods and you will see. In 1924 by John Logi Baird was the birth of the television was discovered by man and it was not too long before households would be invaded by the television tube. When we view television, we observe the creativity of images that reflect society, nature, disasters, evil acts, spiritual acts, love and joy and peace and so many other things in this modern and contemporary society of this world today. We used a single channel with one small antenna used to get the network in place or rather to remove distorted images from the screen to see clearly. The majority of times just putting on the right amount of aluminum foil, then angle it or just bump it would make it alright. It is interesting that those that create movies or film have a notch for creating spectacular breath taking scenes that are remarkable in Godly ways and some less thoughtful. However, they are able to manifest the character, thoughts and images of those on camera expressing reality of the family, community, society, and the world not to mention multiple challenges. You must have an anchored mind to accomplish those things that exceed the normal success. With television a character is anchored in his or her character in order to become that temporary character who in turn affects the society with that particular skit and scene. It is in the mind where we focus our artistic ability and talents for the gain of Christ service giving Him the glory or self gain and glory. The choice and responsibility is each person's own decision and desired choice.

There are an abundance of Hollywood actors, writers, dancers, and singers and just so many people desiring to be a member to contribute to the big blockbuster part. The ability to make film and to be so real in true art form and expression leaves one with the thought of blessing God back. God loves those who love Him back. The point here is that if you have the talent to express movies, use it for the kingdom of God. Make movies that will be sketch images in your mind and the heart of man. God can use any process that He wants to reveal. In His creation, He reminds us that He is a God of fruitfulness. He spoke in Genesis the command of being fruitful and multiplying.

A NEW THOUGHT LIFE

The mind of Christ is the only true and permanent security for life and as a witness for Jesus Christ. Power thoughts that you have in the spirit can anchor you in the Lord. This anchoring is a permanent anchor. It will make the difference in your everyday walk with people you meet. Most people think about receiving blessings all day long even in bad circumstances. The fact that we have the ability to think is one of God's ultimate blessings. God gave us a mind to use and to use it to full capacity. The power to think with a mind of Christ and that's the blessing. The mind of Christ is the ultimate blessing because there is no other mind as Holy and powerful. So in reality we should continue in a mind and heart of praise and acknowledge His many blessings. It is best done in the mind of Christ. There are many reasons that people should have anchored blessings on their mind. One is that the mind of Christ takes your mind to new dimensions of thinking. Secondly, the mind of Christ keeps you from evil thinking and fear. Third, it keeps you in a state of humility. Forth, it helps you to walk in joy unspeakable. Five, it continues to mold you in sanctification and true holiness. Six, it brings you into a state of blessedness. Seven, you can walk in the authority of Christ. My God, those are seven key principles that will help you understand why you should receive Jesus Christ as Savior and allow Him to be your Lord. Eight, your worship becomes true worship in Spirit and in Truth because you are under the influence of the Holy Spirit. Now that is something to rejoice about. You see I am a witness that Jesus is on my mind. That is one reason I decided to write this book. Why not be witness to someone else about the King of Kings, the Lord of Lords who saved my undone soul and delivered me from my wretchedness. When I think of His goodness my soul rejoices in the Lord. When you look at life circumstances all around you, just have Christ like power thoughts. Speak the word in those power thoughts. If a circumstance arises, tell it greater is He in me than He that is in the world. Tell your circumstance that I am more than a conqueror in Christ Jesus. If the circumstance persists, tell it no weapon formed against me shall prosper. With the mind of Christ you just might have to preach to yourself under the influence of the Holy Spirit of course.

THE MIND OF CHRIST DWELL IN YOU

Philippians 2:5 Let this mind be in you, which was also in Christ Jesus: Who, being in the form of God, thought it not robbery to be equal with God: But made himself of no reputation, and took upon him the form of a servant, and was made in the likeness of men; And being found in fashion as a man, he humbled himself, and became obedient unto death, even the death of the cross.

Jesus shows us ultimate humility. He has an amazing attitude about things. But I believe He is showing us something in our thought life as well. He is showing us even in the thought life that our attitudes matter. The way you think is what you see in your life. God already see better than we do. God sees the best in your lives but too many people act blind and faithless. We need to start believing and expecting our blessings that are in store and available from the Lord. God has treasures laid up for us in heaven for our lives right now. God has blessings that we desire. We should never let the enemy or any person tell us that we are limited in God's blessings. God can bless us from the fears of our lives that keep us down from being prosperous to a palace life style. God can fulfill any dream you ever had according to His will of course. We need to expect things from God who is bigger than anyone else and any problem you had or will face. If you keep the fact that you are highly blessed and highly favored in Christ on your mind, you can move mountains in your life to get to your other blessings. You do not have to lay down yourself and quit because of somebody else's mind or opinions or the enemy attacks. You are you perfectly designed by the power of the Most High God, Jesus our rock. Tell anybody that asks you of the blessings in power and authority of the Lord. Jesus helps us to think clearly and have an open heart about our lives and the situation we find ourselves in. Thinking is absolutely one of the most important things we must do if not the most.

BLESSINGS ON MY MIND

God wants us to sustain the attitude of blessings on the mind. Your mind should tell you at all times that you reign with the Father in Heaven, the king of kings, lord of lords. One of the first steps in discussing the mind is to understand what the capabilities of the mind entail and who the designer of it is. We know that God is the designer and this mind is unlimited with God. God designed and enables it to function. The next thing is to ask why is the mind so important. What impact will the mind have on my life? In the natural state the mind is a series of nerves and pulses that take in all information and processes it in various ways, some fast, some reasonably fast and some slower than others. It has the ability to function in capacities that are unlimited only to the designer our Lord. The mind is automatically and systematically designed to function in a capacity with unlimited capabilities to a degree of the will of God that He alone allows because He is the creator and designer of it. However, to do the will of God in the Spirit, it must be converted into the spiritual state for operational and receptive purposes by God. Sometimes it seems like the mind is a mind of its own as we say, but that is so far from the truth. Only carnality and evil can attack you and cause you to think that way. If you are not careful, it will take off on you in many directions or paths because it has not been converted and the devil attacks it and desires to sift your mind as wheat little by little. Sometimes it seems that it can control itself, but do not be fooled or tricked, that is the devil. God helps you to have full control of your mind. But that is not true because there is a force behind the mind and there is a designer who shaped, wired it with special intellect and knowledge, with special individual mind patterns and with the ability to be a genius. God is the only true designer of the mind who can direct it in its proper function and capacity. You have to accept Christ to operate in the spirit realm. You must also know that there is another spiritual process that can rob you of your mind if not converted. The enemy will get into your mind if you are not converted and leave it wide open for entry for more of his demonic spirits. You want the mind of Christ to posses your mind and take over.

BATTLE THINGS OF THE MIND

It is our Lord who enables us to war against the things contrary to His word. We battle things by His might because He always wins. We war against things that attack at the root and surface of the mind. The enemy seeks to steal and rob our minds daily. If you really want to talk about battles of the mind, look at any character in the Bible and you will see that the enemy seems not to give up until the end. If people could see this picture of the mind and thing of the awesome power God used to make the minds of all of His people in creation. His man's mind is different from the animal kingdom or wild life creative minds. Just the thought of Him thinking on making my mind blesses my heart with overwhelming thanksgiving. It sends me in a state of praising His Holy name. "I will bless the Lord at all times, His praise shall continually be in my mouth."

Another scripture that refers to a Christ like mind is: Colossians 3:1-3 If then you were raised with Christ, seek those things which are above, where Christ is, sitting at the right hand of God. Set your mind on things above, not on things on the earth. For you died and your life is hidden with Christ in God.

ROOTED WITH HUMILITY AND OBEDIENCE

Our thinking helps us with the right attitude. It helps condition our minds for the edification and exaltation for the Kingdom of God. The right thinking and the right attitude helps us make the appropriate decision because we find ourselves making a decision that will follow us the rest of our lives. Ultimately the decision we make is monitored by God and He alone can allow it but you made the choice. Every circumstance is the result of some form of choice. Jesus made a decision based off of many things but one was because of thinking under the influence of humility and obedience. In fact, His entire life and ministry focus was to have an attitude of humility and trust toward His Father's mission for Him. Jesus knew what to do and when to do it. He knew what to address and when to address. He was so careful with humility because of His love for all people and at the same time He was training His disciples to be deliverers of the gospel to all the world. He was training them to be witnesses. Jesus, our Lord, saved the entire human race because of His humility toward His Father and all people. His Humility took Him to the cross, the grave and resurrected Him from the dead. He had the Father and love on His mind at all times. His demonstration of love and humility has taken us places because He put things into perspective and in action.

A SERVANTS MIND

Jesus took on Himself the form of a servant. His heart was a servant's heart. He came to serve and not to be served. The actions of Jesus are so gracious, merciful and remarkable in such that even the human mind wonders in amazement of such abounding love. Jesus blessed our minds to be like His. He said Let this mind be in you. He

36

spoke it meaning that the attitude of His mind can be in believers. Jesus is even telling those that are unbelievers that they can have the same mind if they just accept His redemptive power of the cross and the grave. Jesus wants us to be blessed in our humility toward Him and others, blessed in obedience, and blessed because of the cross. He wants our minds to have the same attitude He took upon the cross. Many people have beautiful minds and high I.Q. He wants us to use what we have but express it with the best attitude remembering that you are highly blessed with what you have in your mind. Jesus wants us to be like him if we desire to follow Him. Humility brings about a servant mind. A servant's mind and heart must be focused on the kingdom of God. They must be directly in concentration with Jesus and His blessed will. Only God is perfect and He has anointed His servants minds.

A MADE UP MIND

Jesus blessed us with the proper attitudes. Nevertheless, there are people who need God to reverse their thinking when it comes to God and dating. He wants us to take upon ourselves as His people to reflect these attitudes toward our neighbor but first to Jesus Christ. We need to confess these attitudes daily so they will be in the same mind of Christ daily. We need our minds reversed. We need to confess so that we can walk in the same mind and talk in the same mind of Christ. When we walk in these blessed attitudes in our mind, we then make a difference in society. When we reflect these attitudes we make a difference with our love one and with friends and with people we meet. It is then we can help someone to learn of the Lord and be of the Lord and be connected to the family of God. It so interesting that He stated blessed before every condition of His disciples. He wants His disciples to know that they are blessed even when they go through all of those conditions of mourning, hunger and poor spirit, and whatever state of mind. In fact, do not worry about the persecution and the hard times and tough road ahead. You are highly blessed regardless of the persecution you will encounter. Jesus has already blessed us so rejoice as he said and be exceedingly glad: for great is your reward in heaven. What an awesome attitude to have for the kingdom of God. I believe people should shout when they really come to realization of these blessings God has given us. Just say, He blessed me! He blessed me over and over again!!! God keeps on blessing me. Make it your personal statement daily and ask God to bless someone else daily.

THE MIND TO ACHIEVE NEW HEIGHTS

I am reminded of the story of Jabez. The blessing came when he asked to God enlarge his territory. The God we know will withhold no good thing especially with those who love Him and confess His name. In Corinthians, take hold of the mind of Christ the best you know how. Start with total submission and obedience. Communicate with God in His own words. He hears His words. In the mind of Christ there is nothing that you are incapable of achieving if you desire it and God has a purpose for it with you. See also Ephesians 3: 20 now unto him that is able to do exceedingly abundantly above all that we ask or think, according to the power that works in us.

A MADE UP MIND IS WHATS NEEDED

The mind is so essential to the success of life. You mind is what carry you on a daily basis. The bible specifically speaks in James about a double-minded person. Sometimes the mind is stopped in its tracks. When you come under the anointing, it because the Lord has chosen and poured out His Spirit so He can use you. The Holy Spirit is poured out on God's people often like a outpouring of rain nonstop. When the outpouring happens, you will have a made up mind to glorify God. *JOEL 2: 28-29 And it shall come to pass afterward That I will pour out My Spirit on all flesh; Your sons and your daughters shall prophesy, Your old men shall dream dreams, Your young men shall see visions. And also on my menservants and on my maidservants I will pour out my spirit in those days.*

CHAPTER 4

A MAN AFTER GOD'S OWN HEART

1 Samuel 13:14

1 Samuel 13:14 But now thy kingdom shall not continue:
the LORD hath sought him a man after his own heart, and
the LORD hath commanded him to be captain over his people, because
thou hast not kept that which the LORD commanded thee.

When God select men to serve Him to represent Him as Royal Priest and witnesses on earth, He is not looking for perfection in that man nor that woman. God is looking for men that will accept Him as Lord of their lives. He is looking for ordinary people that He can use as willing vessels. God is looking for someone whose heart He can connect with as they walk in obedience. God is looking for Men with the kind of attitude and heart David had surrendered to God in repentance. God is looking for someone who can walk in faith and trust Him to lead and guide them. King David was anointed King as a young man when God sent Samuel the prophet to Jesse's house. Early on in King David's life God had already observed his heart as a young shepherd boy that fought off lions and bears to protect his Father's flock. Since the young David could demonstrate obedience to his biological father, surely this would please God. Certainly He would be obedient to God, the father in heaven. Keep in mind that David was under God's observation as he tended his father's sheep. This same David as a young man stood up for the entire Israel, God's Army against the Philistine Army and their popular and favorite giant, Goliath. Regardless of how big and intimidating the giant was David still went up against Goliath and killed him. David proved Himself being under God's anointing. King David had a bold and courageous heart. He fought many battles for God and remained obedient. His sin against another man Uriah the Hittite and sleeping with Bathsheba caused Him to repent with his heart to God.

Although, he had the heart to slay giants, he still needed God to fix his heart. So he cried out in Psalm 51 for help so God could clean his heart from sin. David was a man after God's on heart because he went with sincerity of heart to God. God knows if you are serious about Him. You can be a man after God's own heart today. King David had a strong belief in God's power to forgive sin. God knew that David would be obedient to Him in whatever He asked of him according to His will. (Acts 13:22). In addition as you will read shortly, King David, the once Giant Slayer had a repentant heart.

GOD LOOKS AT THE HEART

It used to be that no one could check your heart condition in the most accurate way. Make no mistake about it, God looks at the heart and knows every beat of it. God knows what is inside our heart. No one has ever in history been able to count every heart beat that man has daily and in a life time but God. Your heart condition counts in every possible way because it has something to do with the heart beat as well. A dysfunctional heart will not beat properly or may not beat at all. Any damage could lead to catastrophic results. We need someone who can fix any damage to the heart at any time; He who specializes in heartbeats. There are new capabilities that assist now in determining how many heartbeats a man can have in one single day or even in a minute. But it still may not be as accurate as your body unless the machine is perfectly designed to be with you everywhere and each second of your life. It may be also impossible to measure the stress of the heart as it operates on various occasions and places and fractions of seconds. There are also machines that are used to replace the human heart called the artificial heart. Scientist has also developed a machine called the plastic tube heart that can serve as a substitute for the heart for its span of life. The heart is a blessed component of the body given by God. It is critical to have a heart functioning properly. What is so amazing about the heart is that God is the controller of every beat of the heart. Every beat is operated by God. People that have not accepted Jesus as Savior have difficulty with their heart conditions. The reason God is not controlling your heart even though He designed it but He desires that you accept Him inside of your heart. Then He alone monitors every heart beat in the spirit. You will walk with Him in every beat of your heart.

GOD ANCHOR MY HEART

An Anchored heart is a heart filled with the Holy Spirit. It is a heart that desires and surrenders totally to God for guidance in the spirit for everyday life. An anchored heart is a heart that is unshakable by anything. If you are connected to Jesus, then nothing will separate you from His unfailing love. In my military career, I had to install anchor systems for bridges to function at its peak. If these anchor systems would have let go then the ability to support and cross all of the military heavy tanks and vehicles would fail and prove to be a disaster. Anchors keep the bridge from shifting and add tonnage of support. It is much like the London Bridge and all bridges that require anchoring throughout the world. If the anchoring of those bridges fail, traffic would cease and many fatalities could occur. The mission would be jeopardized and not accomplished. We must have God as our anchor in our life. Our hearts must be anchored in His word daily to sustain this spirit walk.

One of the most gifted specialists of our day is the medical surgeon. In this particular case it would be the heart surgeon. The heart surgeon has the skills beyond the average surgeon in respect to heart treatment. It is vitally important to understand the debts of what the heart surgeon does. One thing we do know that in his field of expertise, he handles the heart, the most precious and delicate part of the human anatomy. He knows exactly where to cut to repair blood vessels. He knows the in and outs of the heart chambers. He knows what is health and not healthy for the heart. He knows what is clogging the arteries of the heart. He is the one to go to when heart disease and heart attacks happen in a moment notice. He knows what to look for in an x-ray of your heart. He can sum up exactly what is necessary for you to live a healthy lifestyle. The fact of the matter is that God gave the surgeon his gifts of examining and operating on the heart. However, there is not greater Surgeon than the Lord Himself who knows the very makeup, design and where it came from. Our Father is the architect of the heart. He invented, design, sculptured and put life in the heart. In Genesis, the word tells us that God breathed the breath of life into man. It was the heart of man that God breathed into. It was every fabric of the human anatomy that God breathed inside of man. Thank God that He has more knowledge than the human surgeons. Although thank God for the surgeons on earth that he gifted to do a good work. However, we know that God is the miracle maker of the heart situations and circumstances. Thank God that he knows how to cover the heart. Conditions may occur in the wicked way, but we are covered in the blood of the Lamb and the blood is applied to our hearts as well as our entire makeup, in spirit and body.

A SECOND CHANCE TO CHANGE YOUR HEART

There was a man who had a heart condition living next door but you could never tell that He had a condition. One day after seven months of passing by my house even though he lived next door, he stopped and talked to me a while. If he had not dropped his documents out of his suitcase to the ground we probably would have missed that moment of talking. That very moment gave us a chance to get to know something about one another. I stopped and tried to help him pick up as many as possible pieces of paper before they flew away. He said thanks and mentioned something about if He had to pick all of the paper up, his heart would probably give out. I thought he was referring to the pain inside of the heart. But he was referring to the quilt he felt about have to accept the divorce his wife was filing for over an extra marital relationship that he had committed. Well, it turned out the he never knew the Lord as well. In fact, He as an executive chairperson of a lager firm was becoming attracted to a cult. That day he asked me a simple question. How can I get out of all of this mess? I told him it is easier than you think. Now there will be a few rough spot along the path. But you can make it through. I told him about what King David did to one of his generals who was fighting a war on his behalf. But what he did after was the only way to be restored and healed properly.

David listened to a prophet named Nathaniel who told him the truth about himself. Afterwards, David repented to the Lord with his entire heart, believing it deeply in spirit that God had forgiven Him and that He could hold on to the hand of God. *A*ccording to Dobson et al., (1994) David addresses God in Hebrew (Elohim) because this in the eyes of God to him announce how unworthy King David is that he does not utter the name Jehovah. *In Psalm 51:10: He said those word, Create in me a clean heart, O Lord and renew a right spirit within me. Do not cast me away from Your presence, And do not take Your Holy Spirit from me. Restore to me the joy of Your salvation, And uphold me by Your generous Spirit (Dobson, et al.,1994)*

God wants us to walk with a new heart that reflects the heart of Jesus Christ. Ask God to do a spiritual makeover with your heart. Turn from your old ways because you are a child of God so walk by faith in your spiritual heart. Show off your new heart to at least 1 million people. Send hundreds or thousands the word of God each week through email or I-Phone

A REPENTANT HEART

David said create in me a clean heart, O Lord and renew a right spirit within me. Everyone on earth needs a clean heart. No not one person is exempt from the need of a clean heart because we were born into sin by Adam and Eve. David acknowledged to the Lord that his heart had a condition other than clean that made his behavior unacceptable in the eyes of the Lord. What a difference it makes to just make one stop in an effort to get one person to repent and accept Jesus as Lord and Savior.

Do you have a heart of repentance? God desires a heart that will turn away from wickedness and honor Him by living Godly lifestyles. We must make it a daily priority in our lives to ask God for repentance when we fall in temptation or any traps or entanglement. No one is exempt! You will need to repentant daily in this life.

God is so loving and merciful in all His ways. Our father created us with a heart that beats with life and there is no other component of the body like it or that can compare. The heart is a permanent part of your life. You wish you could see it and handle it. But The Lord our God gave us that heart to know him and to love Him along with everyone else in this Earth. It is amazing that He put such a small size muscle material inside of our bodies that beats according to His time and design. Man did not create the heart. God created it and shaped it like a potter molds and shapes clay models. He is the potter of our heart. He simply designed every measurement and component of the heart. He made beats of our hearts and controls it daily. If it were not for our Lord Jesus our hearts would not beat. Therefore we would not have life. That in itself is so profound because the heart by God's standard had become wicked before God in the beginning and in so many people lives. God speaks of that in the story of Noah. That is exactly why He had Noah to build an ark. The heart of man meant that much and still does to God. The heart is the center of where God places love and life. Genesis 6.

A HEART OF EXPECTATION

All people have a certain expectation of their heart. The first thing for sure each day we automatically expect for our hearts to function. We just know that it will work through the night and through the day. We expect to wake up with a perfect heart, not skipping a beat. We have a mindset that never even thinks about our heart stopping and we should keep thinking and believing it as long as we live. Keep a positive and faith filled attitude in our heart. We need to expect in our heart to move beyond limits and have new attitude. Too often people remain the same, stop being idle and become aggressive with love to get Jesus in your life. Grab hold of your blessing in Jesus Christ and let old issues become a thing of the past. Press for the goal line and score blessings of a lifetime. You lifetime blessing might be service to the Lord. Some might be to simply crossover from the dark side to the seeing the light of Christ Jesus shine in your life. For most, it has to be to be with Him eternally, to be pulled up in the air and reign with Him. So do not let your expectation be diminished because of someone talked you out of it or their opinion of you stopped you in your tracks or you needed in our mind someone's approval. Stop thinking like that. God has already approved you and He thinks highly of you and no demon in hell can stop His powerful thinking and approving for appointing you for His purpose and showering you in blessings. From now on expect the best because you are a child of the Most High.

OVERCOME EVIL WITH GOOD

The Bible clearly tells us in Matthew 15:19 For out of the heart proceed evil thoughts, murders, adulteries, fornications, thefts, false witness, blasphemies:. Many people need a need a heart transplant. The right surgeon could do the job and make the person all new in many cases. There is only one who can do. God encourages us through Apostle Paul in Romans 12:21 Be not overcome of evil, but overcome evil with good. I thank God that he allows us to repent as well of our sins. Repentance means turning away from sin, the old lifestyle. The best medicine for the heart is Jesus and the power of repentance. His heart must be a repentant heart. David made a mistake that many people make in society today. But he made a statement through prayer to God also. In his prayer, he simply repented from the heart. Pray with your heart in the spirit when you repent. You can do it because it is the love of God that places the power of His Holy Spirit over our lives as He plants His spirit inside our hearts and minds. We are anchored in His blessings through His Spirit in our hearts.

Our father in Heaven loves a repentant heart like King David's who was anointed. He had a sincere heart when he asks the Lord to clean his heart. He trusted that God would forgive and bless him when he repent and fasted through the power of the Holy Spirit. He knew it because He said do not take away your Holy Spirit. It means that God blesses those that sincerely repent from the heart. King David knew that God's Holy Spirit is where our blessings come from such as the power of forgiveness in repentance. When you repent, God sees it as you turning your heart over to him to fix all the corruption and brokenness. He cleanses the heart and makes our heart new. Each day it is only the Holy Spirit that can take things that are not good away from the heart each day. Don't limit want the Holy Spirit can do for you. The Apostle Paul wrote in Romans 12:20, "Overcome evil with good" Focus on good things to dwell in your heart. Study good things to put on your mind. Meditate on the word of God and He will lead you through to have the victory every time.

A NEW HEART

God speaks to us in Ezekiel 36:26-27 saying, *I will give you a new heart and put a new spirit within you; I will take the heart of stone out of your flesh and give you a heart of flesh. I will put My Spirit within you and cause you to walk in my statutes, and you will keep my judgments and do them.*

In this chapter I believe it is important to mention the love of God which is shed abroad by the Holy Spirit. Our father is so rich in love and tender care. Roman 8:38-39 the Apostle Paul writes for I am persuaded that neither death nor life, nor angels nor principalities nor powers, nor things present nor things to come, nor height nor depth, nor any other created thing, shall be able to separate us from the love of God which is in Christ Jesus our Lord. So in this love of God nothing can separate you from His love. Sure you may make bad choices or decisions but His love is so unlimited it covers a multitude of sin. The scripture also tells us that while we were yet sinners, He still loved us. Most of us understand that there is the sin of blasphemy that God said that will never be forgiven. Now that is what He said. God is real and He knows about us. God will not go against His word. Blasphemy has no expression of love; it is only hate and a form of evil thinking. More, importantly, He is reminded us to tell all people to take Him serious as God and do not profane my name. Do not go against my name. Do not defile me before anything. Blasphemy is any form of evil against God. It is a direct attack on Him. Tell a friend that He is Lord and Sovereign. Nothing is greater than Him. He is the Alpha and Omega.

CHAPTER 5

THE SOUL AND SPIRIT MAN

Ezekiel 18:4, Matthew 22:37

Reverse the Tide: God wants all of his people to surrender their soul and spirit to him alone and no one else.

The soul is the mind, will and emotion. Be careful do not let the enemy rob you. Do not allow the enemy to rob you of your soul. If you know you need to get on the road to heaven instead of being on the road to hell, get Jesus Christ in your life today. Stop waiting! He has to power to change your soul and spirit man. Reverse your lifestyle today, meaning change directions in 180 degree change. In many cases, you might find yourself reverse actions, backing up from things that tempt you and test you as a Christian. The power is with the Holy Spirit. He will help you. Give your soul to Jesus Christ, King of Kings and Lord of Lords! Let Him know today. The Lord looks at the man who reverences Him. That is one way of knowing how you stand with God. How you treat God and respect determines more than you can even think. It is a blessing to know that God owns the souls of men. But we need to make very clear that God allows each person to learn and know that your choice is your choice. One of the reasons why God sends His preacher out to preach is to spread the word of God so that all people will be delivered. He is serious about every living soul. They belong to Him. Today reverse your soul direction. In other words, if you know that you are headed to hell, ask Jesus to come into your life. Most people need this blunt conversation because they keep doing the same thing-blowing Jesus off! You will need Him. Reversing your soul means that if the enemy has a grip on your life right now, you can change the directions by turning yourself over to Jesus Christ. Soul reversing means start living for Jesus Christ. Break away from the things that have you so enticed and keep you away from serving God. Break away from a spirit of un-forgiveness.

Someone hurt you so bad and have not let go of it. Jesus wants us to let go of all of those things. But you have allowed your soul to be entangled with it. Give it Jesus today. Go to the altar and give up this Sunday at church. Go your bedroom and get on your knees and pray. God hears your prayer. Become a servant of the Most High God and watch your life change and the benefits increase and the blessings multiply. God is not in competition. Nevertheless he will out do the evil one every moment, every day of your life. Turn your spirit man and soul over to God.

EVERY SOUL IS GOD'S

Ezekiel 18:4 For every living soul belongs to me, the father as well as the son both alike belong to me. The soul who sins is the one who will die

Everyone needs to understand that the God of this creation and love owns everything including your soul and mine. If God did not own our soul, then the devil would own it permanently. He already cannot wait to take it from you and poison your life. God wants to give the good life plus more abundantly life.

Ezekiel 18:20 The soul who sins is the one who will die. The son will not share the quilt of the father, nor will the father share the quilt of the son. The righteousness of the righteous man will be credited to him; and the wickedness of the wicked will be charged against him.

How do you submit your soul to the Lord? Listen to this scripture below. Love God with all of you soul, mind and spirit. You just need to let go and let God. Let God be the center of your life. He will bless you. He will renew you.

Jesus said in *Matthew 22:37 you shall love the Lord your God with all your heart, with all your soul, and with your entire mind. This is the first and great commandment. And the second is like it: You shall love your neighbor as yourself.*

48

The Solution is your power Father to release me to love my neighbor. I know now that I have to use the same faith you gave to your servant Joseph when He knew that his brothers were against him in his household. Lord I pray for Janet also to forgive me. I thank you today Father that you redeemed me from sin's attack. Today I will trust in the Lord with all my heart and soul and mind. You are worthy O'Lord to be praise forever and ever.

MY SOUL IS GOD'S

We really must be cautious with all five parts that Jesus pointed out. He uses these as the most sensitive parts of our lives. He knows on a daily basis these three require nourishment and it is also convenient that there are three in agreement. They must be agreement as the trinity. Jesus specifically points out the soul. He said that we should love Him with all of our soul. What is the soul? The soul is man's very conscience. You are aware of who you are with your soul. Some people like to think of the soul as the inner man connected to the spirit man inside you and that is okay. The scripture says that God created man and breathe the breath of life in him and he became a living soul. Soul actually is one of the first acts of the being blessed because God brought life into man by activating his soul. We see clearly why we must be connected to the Lord Himself. Well first of all He started creation that way. It was never a question as to who fashioned the soul of man or who put together the soul man. Think of it this way. Have you ever heard of an invisible man? You can see the outer lining of that man or women to know that they exist and are made up. Another blessing in the process of giving man a living soul is that the Lord allowed man to make choices with the soul he gave to man. We can either anchor our soul in Christ Jesus or we can anchor our souls in Satan. The scripture plainly tells us that we cannot serve two masters. The scripture also requires us to love Him with all of our soul.

SOUL WIINNING

God will win souls by using those who believe in Jesus Christ. He desires that we go forth with an attitude to win. Don't let up on people because they seem like they do not care. Ask the Holy Spirit to put you in overdrive if you have to. You will need to ask because some people will make you feel like you are stuck and can do anything. You come out of your spiritual rut as well so you can move for God.

The power to win is His power. When you anchor you soul it means many things. One thing for sure it means that service for the Lord will become you primary priority in life. So there is a raging war going on. The issue at hand is that so many people war against the enemy on his turf and the territory that you allow him to possess. Most people saw the movie Ghost with the actor playing as a fortune teller and spirit intervener. In the mind people believe that the enemy truly has turf and territory. If you would like to call Hell or Hades his turf you can. But you are still giving him too much credit because even Hell belongs to God. God made it for evil to be separated from Him. The enemy has been placed their but his rent is about to expire. He will soon be sent to the lake of fire for eternity. See you do not have to fear evil. It is just like the word says; God has not given you the spirit of fear but of power, love and a sound mind.

PUT YOUR SOUL IN HIS HAND

Ezekiel 18:20 the soul who sins is the one who will die. The son will not share the quilt of the father, nor will the father share the quilt of the son. The righteousness of the righteous man will be credited to him, and the wickedness of the wicked will be charged against him.

SOUL SUMBMISSION

Jack wonders about His soul since His co-workers asked him about salvation. Jack really did not have an answer. Now His mind is completed on it. Somewhere in the corner of his mind he keeps on thinking about it. He knew that his wife always talked about the Lord and being baptized and he heard the word saved. So many of his friends always talk about the Lord did this and the Lord did that but he was still confused because they did not act like Christians in his mind. He thought that Christians were suppose be perfect and not drink and club at night or anytime but he has been seeing the opposite and this is what kept him away.

Psalms 27:1-2 The Lord is my light and my salvation; who shall I fear? The Lord is the strength of my life; of whom shall I be afraid?

Psalms 34:8 Oh' taste and see that the Lord is good; blessed is the man who trusts in Him!

POWER IN MY SOUL

Regina Golden attended church today. She was impressed with the music because it moved her tremendously throughout the service. She had tears rolling down her eyes and was in awe of the touching of the anointing that Sunday morning of July 1, 2005. In her mind she could not understand what just happen to her in the fullness of understanding. That night she spoke with her husband about her experience in church. Jack did not know much about what was happening. He had attended for a while. He had a bad experience and did not want to return. Regina thought about how she had just been out there and feeling empty in the past, even as early as yesterday and it affected her mind and relationship. Her thought in church and at home was that I need Jesus to anchor my soul in His hand.

The truth is that she told herself about it, heard herself even after God spoke to her but continued in sin. In her mind the more she meditated on it and talked about it to herself and even to Loretta Myles her best friend, she sank deeper and deeper. That is exactly what the sin life does to you. It causes you to sink in sin that creeps in your life on a sneak. The more she talked about her, her resentment grew. To add to the matter, Janet had gained a new male friend who looked better than her male friends. She even forgot the fact that she was married for a moment. Regina had discovered something through all of this. She finally realized that she does not have a real problem with her co-worker. She knows that the problem is sin. Her question to God is, Lord how do I get free from the sin of jealousy and bitterness in my life? Release from feeling this terrible way.

CHAPTER 6

INNER MAN'S TEMPLE

The Apostle Paul said in I Corinthians 3:16 Do you not know that you are the temple of God and that the Spirit of God dwell in you?

REVERSE THE TIDE: Attend Sunday Worship service in God's temple and allow Jesus to come into your life and fill your body with power. He desires to dwell inside you. Today do not allow anything else inside you; however asks Jesus to come into your heart.

MAKE HIM THE CENTER OF YOUR LIFE

The inner man's temple is your body with the spirit man inside of you. Your body is supposed to be God's temple. God dwells on the inside of you. Reverse all of your thinking and get to God's temple for worship. In other words, go to church this Sunday and worship the Lord Jesus. When we think of temples we think of a huge building with a cross on the top of it and people on the inside and everyone should be holy. We often think that everyone will be walking with crosses in their hands. It is a good thing that we walk with a cross to be reminded of His sacrifice for mankind. The presence of the Lord dwells in buildings that are temples and God can dwell wherever He wants to. Most people visit buildings on Sunday or throughout the week, months and years to worship Him in the sanctuary. God manifest His love in people on earth whenever they are calling on the name of the Lord. He said to call on Him and He will be there. He created them for his pleasure and in His people He reveals He amazing love and his plan for our lives.

God gave us this vessel to be used by Him. This vessel is a temple for His Spirit to dwell in. Everyone was designed to be a receiver of the power of His love. Love is the example and proof of God in our lives. With your body being a temple for God, He desires that you keep your body in good health, avoid drugs and foods that cause problems associated with disease and decline of health. God our Lord also wants His people to avoid fornication and adultery. The anchor is that your body is God's. When you violate your body, you violate God. However, the fact remains also that God uses your temple as a witness for others even when you fall. You are a fallen temple that God can rebuild anytime. Jesus told the Pharisees that I will destroy this temple and build up in three days. He was referring to His death, burial and resurrection. You are a reconstructed temple when you were delivered from crack, cocaine, and meth and any other drug addiction. Even now you can be a walking temple who witnesses to God's people about His anchoring power. His magnificent anchoring power never leaves you or forsakes you. He will get His glory no matter what. It is fixed in His plan even your life itself.

USE ME LORD!

Ask the Lord the help you to stop moving forward in the things not of God but reverse the tide and start walking by faith in Jesus Christ. There are things in your life that are heavier than you think but you know that it's been weighing you down. Please understand that God used Saul a murderer to become one of the greatest men ever in history. Even in the darkest and most evil moments of Saul, God saw fit to change him. Yes God can change anybody. He changed Saul to Paul on the road to Damascus. Paul was transformed instantly once he met Jesus on the road to Damascus. The main point to make here is that once he arrived to Ananias, God announced to him that Paul was a chosen vessel. This is another way of viewing the importance of the temple. God sent this temple and vessel on missions that no other man had accomplished in life. One major point to make is that once Saul who is now Paul met Jesus on the road, his soul was changed and anchored to the Lord from that point on. He spent His life as a servant of the Lord.

DON'T REVERSE YOUR GODLY IMAGE

God also made us in the image of Him. Genesis spells it out. He made man in the image and then made the woman. He gave them bodies from the dust and with his power transformed these bodies with skin, still dirt. He breathed the breath of life in the first man, Adam. So then it all centers back to Adam's body and choices. He was the lead man on earth because he was the first man on earth. Later he speaks of being fruitful and multiplying. He is referring to children. Your body must be taken care of. He is also referring to spirit multiplication. He expects for us to carry our temples or bodies in a way that will honor Him. We are blessed because the Holy Spirit resides in us according to the scripture.

We also need to be reminded that Jesus spoke very clearly of His body being a temple. He told the Pharisees and Sadducees that His body would be torn down but built again, speaking of His resurrection. They were confused because they understood the church and the temple to be the actual true and only place to worship. That is absolutely not true. Jesus wants us to have Him on the inside of our hearts which leads to the inside of our lives to worship Him. Jesus must be in your heart to have true worship. Matthew 7

THE LAMBS TEMPLE

Revelation 21:22-23. John says, but I saw no temple in it, for the Lord God Almighty and the Lamb is its temple. The city had no need of the sun or of the moon to shine in it for the glory of God illuminated it. The Lamb is its light. And the nations of those who are saved shall walk in its light, and the kings of the earth bring their glory and honor into it.

God loves the holy temple of His people for He alone shines through that temple so every man, woman, and child has a precious body that has the Spirit of God shining through them. It is almost as if He makes our bodies inside prepared as a holy temple for Him and at the same time reflects the New Jerusalem.

WRITTEN IN THE LAMBS BOOK

Revelations 21:27 but there shall by no means enter it anything that defiles, or causes an abomination or a lie, but only those who are written in the Lamb's book of life.

Is your name written in the lamb's book of life? In order for your name to be written in the book of life, you must be born again into the kingdom of God. You must be a true child of God who worships Him alone. We must be one of His who loves Him back. We must devote ourselves to Him the way He planned. We must be that child of God that walks in obedience and spirit. We who are written in the book know Him and reverence Him in the fullness of joy and spirit. We are surrender to Him and are the Saints that He adores and is pleased with in service. God does not make it difficult for us. It is just a matter of surrender in freedom to God.

HIS THRONE ESTABLISHED FOREVER

2 SAMUEL 7: 14-17 I will be his father, and he shall be my son. If he commit iniquity, I will chasten him with the rod of men, and with the stripes of the children of men: But my mercy shall not depart away from him, as I took it from Saul, whom I put away before thee. Your house and your kingdom will endure forever before me; your throne will be established forever. Nathan reported to David all the words of this entire revelation.

David wanted to build God a temple but God had other plans. God promises to establish David's house forever. But David would not be the one to build it. He was still blessed. But God wanted his son to build it. David had blood on his hands.

Your temple is special to God, which is your body.

CHAPTER 7

LIVING IN BLESSINGS AND PARADISE

Deuteronomy 28

WHAT MAKES YOU WANT TO LIVE WITH JESUS FOREVER?
LIVE A LIFE OF BLESSINGS AND PARADISE.

REVERSE THE TIDE: Reverse you living again. If you are not
taking time out with your wife, the woman you love, life can be a
challenge and you are making it difficult. Live life like you are in
Paradise.

You have complete authority over your life because God has your
life in the palm of His hand. That is good to know and have confidence
in. Living on Paradise Island is the picture most people dream of
living. The first thing is to know Jesus and know then that you are
blessed. You miss blessings because you fail to have a relationship.
For those that have accepted Jesus Christ as Lord, they know what
blessings are and receive them. They have a real relationship. Paradise
for many people is the perfect home with all the necessities and
accommodations of a beach view filled with the perfect picture of
glistening blue clear water, back deck with candles lit, perfect skies
and waters with the exotics touch of trees and the view from a few
stories high balcony. This is also with service in your room delivered
everyday of your life with every meal tasting perfect. People who want
a paradise lifestyle desire the best of service and materials that money
can buy. It is of no concern that paradise is real and people strive for it.
Most people just want a peace fill life without any interruptions and
snags and concerns that eat at their minds. Most people just want to
live life and want for others to live their lives to the fullest and enjoy
all the blessings of the Lord. Can you imagine just eating at the table
with a buffet unlimited with exotic fruit, various food, dancers and
trained musicians that hit all the key notes perfectly with a melody

entering your heart and mind, soothing the soul and spirit. You are at the point of no return in a relaxing place. There is no stopping you from getting what is yours at this point in life.

There are islands that have exactly what you and I are looking for in the best vacation of our lives. Hawaii is definitely one. It is the perfect paradise island. No interruptions, no concerns, no commitments on the outside. There are some unique things about Hawaii: We know that it is popular for the luau in entertainment. It is well known for the coconut trees and so many exotic ocean fruits and sea creatures. It is known to have coral beneath the sea that are remarkable in beauty and design by God. We also know that in the midst of the beauty luxury of a paradise island are volcanoes that can erupt without notice. Surely there are alarms that go off to warn local people. The reality is that it's a risk and the risk is yours. It has another component that could happen and it is called a tsunami. A tsunami is body of water that is triggered by a shift in the earth in the bottom plates of the ocean and cause waves at a height underdetermine that rush the shore lines and wipeout human life.

The reality is that we can still have a blessed life in paradise. God controls the seas and the wind. God controls the fire in the earth and all the volcanoes and the lava within. He also has all of paradise in His hand. We take risk everyday of life. The enemy comes at us often like a storm and even an erupted volcano that tries to sweep us away, but we have an advocate who sits high and looks low and loves us with an everlasting love. His name is Jesus. He gives us hope and comfort reveals the reality of life to us daily.

The reality also is that there are many who are destined to the same life of blessings in pleasure but they never arrive because they allow something or someone to hold them back. For too many people it is a captivity mentality. They are being held captive on the island of evil. Don't you ever let Satan still your joy and peace and the blessings God has laid up for you. You come off of the island of evil to the island of blessings and abundance and prosperity in Christ Jesus. Which do you prefer? Captivity or paradise? Lock up or freedom? The choice is yours. Today ask God to release you from all the pain and suffering and all the blocks from blessings in my life. You see what happens in order to even experience the paradise beyond human nature paradise is to accept Jesus as Lord and Savior. When you accept Him, you are on your way to a pre-paid paradise island trip. When He returns and takes His own with Him, we are good forever. This time you do not have to worry about a return ticket. You do not have to worry about anyone calling you and telling you that a major project is due, the accounting books need to be updated, the business and marketing plan must be written, or an interview for a new job is scheduled for today, mortgage rent is due, money is low, no milk in the refrigerator, spilt Kool-Aid is on the floor, a honey do list must be completed, a gambling debt is due, divorce papers must be signed, you need to appear before your local judge for sentencing, and all concerns will be no longer of yours. For now you are on God's side.

ANOINTED WITH BOLDNESS
FOR GOD'S PURPOSE

We are blessed with the words spoken in this passage: Isaiah 61:1-4 The Spirit of the Lord God is upon me, because the Lord has anointed me to preach good tidings to the poor, He has sent me to heal the brokenhearted, to proclaim liberty to the captives, and the opening of the prison to those who are bound. He sent me to proclaim the acceptable year of the Lord, and the day of vengeance of our God; to comfort all that mourn in Zion, to give them beauty for ashes, the oil of joy for mourning, the garment of praise for the spirit of heaviness; that they may be called trees of righteousness, the planting of the Lord, that He may be glorified.

God wants His word to go forth to set people free from any condition that they are presently in. God desires for us to have a freedom beyond our imagination in every aspect of life. He sets man free from all aspects of captivity. Only the salvation of Jesus Christ in the heart of man can set a man free from captivity. We are blessed to know that God would take the time out of His schedule to set a man free. If you look at all the conditions in your life that are keeping you in captivity and write them down and then ask Jesus to set you free. Then just wait and feel the power of the Lord. He will do it. Tell everyone you know that God set you free from captivity. I like what Isaiah said. He said the spirit of the Lord is upon me. That already signified the great work that Isaiah was about to do with the spirit of the Lord inside of him. See also Luke 4: Jesus said the similar statement

FOR GOD'S PURPOSE

The Solution is your power Father to release me. I know now that I have to use the same faith you gave to your servant Joseph when He knew that his brothers were against him in his household. Lord I pray for Janet also to forgive me. I thank you today Father that you redeemed me from sin but I allow it to attack. Today I will trust in the Lord with all thine

The statement that every Christian loves to here is you will be with me in paradise. It is a blessing to know that Jesus took the thief on the cross next to Him to heaven on His set time. It shows the love of God and why He was on that cross. He blessed us and we still get blessings from that day on to now and throughout eternity.

Every Christian crosses over into God's kingdom by making this simple statement of confession in Romans10:9 according the scripture. This is indeed the ultimate blessing that has power to transform the lives of not only millions of people but all people. This scripture blesses us in that it makes us apart of Jesus because we accepted Him as Lord of our lives. We now have access to all spiritual blessings in heaven because of our new relationship with the Lord. Often in our lives it takes something drastic to accept Jesus as Lord. But do not wait for that kind of invitation. Get the Lord in your life now, today because He has already blessed you every day of your life up to this point. This is your time to accept Jesus as your Lord and continue in His blessings for eternity. Come and get your blessing now and become part of the Kingdom of God. This will make your life feel more meaningful than anything you can ever imagine.

MAKE YOUR CONFESSION PERSONAL

Romans 10:9-10 that if you confess with your mouth the Lord Jesus and believe in your heart that God has raised Him from the dead, you will be saved. For with the heart one believes unto righteousness, and with the mouth confession is made unto salvation.

For anyone who accepts Jesus Christ as Lord and Savior, it is the most joyful and blessed moment of life. This occurs because of your confession life. Nothing can compare to the Spirit of Jesus Christ entering your heart and making over your mind and Spirit in His image. Your confession has taken you into the Kingdom of God. You are a new convert and life will never be the same again. You live for the kingdom of God and His purpose. Your new destiny will be to reign in God's paradise with Him forever. You and I can now announce to the world that salvation is free. You do not have to pay anything for it. No one in existence can purchase such a blessed gift. It was done on Calvary by the blood of the Lamb, Jesus Christ. In Ephesians 2:8, scripture states, for by grace you have been saved through faith, and that not of yourselves; it is the gift of God, not of works, lest anyone should boast.

When we come into God's kingdom he has so many blessings waiting on us that we can't even count. Take a look below at Deuteronomy chapters 11 and 28.

THE SOLE OF YOUR FOOT

TREAD BLESSING

Moses wrote in Deuteronomy 11:24-28 every place on which the sole of your foot treads shall be yours: from the wilderness and Lebanon, from the river, the River Euphrates, even to the Western Sea, shall be your territory. No man shall be able to stand against you; the Lord your God will put the dread of you and the fear of you upon all the land where you tread, just as He has said to you. Behold I set before you blessing and a curse: the blessing, if you obey the commandments of the Lord your God which I command you today; and the curse, if you do not obey the commandments of the Lord your God, but turn aside from the way which I command you today, to go after other gods which you have not known.

Everything in life might not feel like a blessing in paradise experience. But if you obey Him, one thing for sure you get blessings instead of curses. Then the blessings that He gives are like being in paradise if that's how He designed for you. God blessed Joshua to the highest degree. He allowed Him into the promise land. Joshua was obedient to God and so God rewarded Him by allowing Joshua and the people to experience the land of milk and honey. God did not stop with Joshua. He made it available for us today. We can experience the land of milk and honey. We just need to obey His voice and be obedient in His will for our lives. God loves to bless us. He takes pleasure in blessing His people. When you walk in obedience with God, you can be blessed where the sole of your feet touch. No man can stand against you and the blessings that God has for you. Be encouraged today and live a life filled with the blessings that God has granted you and those on the way. The Lord blesses farmers, executives, teachers, preachers, professional athletes, fishermen, missionaries, servants of the Most High, and in those in every category of life. God blessed children and generations to come. He is the God who blesses Jew and Gentile. He wants all of His people to know to take on the attitude of Joshua and obedience in His will and surely you will be highly blessed.

BLESSINGS OVERTAKE ME

Moses wrote in Deuteronomy 28: 1-4"Now it shall come to pass, if you diligently obey the voice of the Lord your God, to observe carefully all His commandments which I command you today, that the Lord your God will set you high above all nations of the earth. And all these blessings shall come upon you and overtake you, because you obey the voice of the Lord. Blessed shall you be in the city, and blessed shall you be in the country. Blessed shall be the fruit of your body, the produce of your ground and the increase of your herds, the increase of your cattle and the offspring of your flocks."

Ephesians 2:8 for by grace we are saved, not of ourselves, not of works, it is the gift of God.

Rev 4:12. In eternal life, we will make it to heaven. We see according to the Apostle John that we can make it to heaven and worship heaven there forever. Those clothed in white raiment bow before His throne.

CHAPTER 8

EVERY SPIRITUAL BLESSING

Ephesian 1:3, Mark 10, Luke 12

GOD WANTS HIS PEOPLE TO KNOW SPIRITUAL BLESSINGS

ANCHOR 8 You have been blessed with all spiritual blessings by the authority of Jesus. Your blessings and possibilities are limitless.

BLESSED WITH EVERY SPIRITUAL BLESSING

In Ephesians 1:3-6, the Apostle Paul says Blessed be the God and Father of our Lord Jesus Christ, who has blessed us with every spiritual blessing in the heavenly places in Christ, just as He chose us in Him before the foundation of the world, that we should be holy and without blame before Him in love, having predestined us to adoption as sons by Jesus Christ to Himself, according to the good pleasure of His will, to the praise of the glory of His grace, by which He made us accepted in the Beloved.

God ensured that we are blessed with every spiritual blessing in heaven and on earth. Psalms 24 tells us that the earth is the Lord's and fullness of it. God does not limit us to His blessings. Our priority in life is not the riches and prosperity of the world. The Bible does remind us that the riches of the wicked are laid up for the righteous. We own much more than what is in the world. We own every spiritual blessing according to God's will. You own more than what is in the natural. The natural really should come easier than what we make it out to be. If every Christian thought about the blessings that He and she really own, they will stop and bless somebody else. Our goal is to please God in love and service and His own specific purpose for each of our lives.

64

REVERSE THE TIDE

We were rich in blessings before the foundation of the earth.

We know this because God created all things so He owns them. They that are of God have an inheritance to what God owns.

REVEALING RICHES!

2 CHRONICLES 29:12-13

God always reveals His blessings through riches in this life and the life to come. God has clearly shown us that He can make a millionaire and billionaire right before our very own eyes. If you ask a millionaire and a billionaire how it feels to be rich. I am sure they will tell you that it is the good life. Most would probably tell you that it is like living in a paradise. Those are good earthly riches. These riches are blessings from God.

Christian riches are from God and they are spiritual and they are Earthly. So then the believer can never be without unless they chose to. Also as long as there are other Christians, a Christians will never be without, should never lack or live in poverty. If you are in poverty and you are around other Christians who can help, then God is on the way to bring you out of that situation. All Christians as a matter of fact, Christians should be willing to bless you because they have an overflow of blessings that need to be given as blessings. You have to believe and then receive it. Listen to what God expressed through His man servant. God, the Father of Jesus Christ has blessed us with every spiritual blessing in the heavenly places. What a magnificent thought to have blessings laid up in heaven all because He is worthy of His word. The word of God has every spiritual blessing in it. If you stay connected to the word of God, your blessings will be revealed as you read it and meditate on it. As you go through each chapter you will see blessings. God wants all of His people to have riches and to be happy with a good healthy and spirit filled life. Jesus even said in His world I came to give you life and to give it to you more abundantly. That is a life without any limits of blessings. We must believe and acknowledge Him.

He established a covenant to bless all of His people. The Lord keeps on reminding us of His blessings in Ephesians chapter 1 verse 18.

Ephesians 1: 18 the eyes of your understanding being enlightened that you may know the hope of His calling, what are the riches of the glory of His inheritance in the saints, and what is the exceeding greatness of His power toward us who believe, according to the working of His mighty power.

Moses says in Deuteronomy 8: 1-18 Every commandment which I command you today you must be careful to observe, that you may live and multiply, and go in and possess the land of which the Lord swore to your fathers. And you shall remember that the Lord your God led you all the way these forty years in the wilderness, to humble you and test you, to know what was in your heart, whether you would keep His commandments or not. So He humbled you, allowed you to hunger, and fed you with manna which you did not know nor did your fathers know, that He might make you know that man shall not live by bread alone; but man lives by every word that proceeds from the mouth of the Lord. Your garments did not wear out on you, nor did your foot swell these forty years. You should know in your heart that as a man chastens his son, so the Lord your God chastens you. Therefore you shall keep the commandments of the Lord your God to walk in His ways and fear him. For the Lord your God is bringing you into a good land, a land of brooks of water, of fountains and springs, that flow out of valleys and hills;

Moses, the man of God reminds the people of the many blessing God had given in the wilderness experience. Moses reminds them that God wants them to keep His commandments. Keeping these commandments will help you multiply and possess the land that God swore to their fathers.

CROSS THAT LINE!

Many people have had an encounter with death or some close call that threaten life. They believed that they died and God allowed them a second chance. This picture similar to the rich man in Luke 16 who had a chance to bless someone else with his riches that God had blessed him with. God is not giving him a second chance in this passage. This rich man was given an opportunity to accept the Lord long before this encounter. Now he wants to speak from the other side to warn his brothers about hell. Imagine what he wanted to say. Maybe it is as simple as don't come here! Whatever you do, do not come to hell. This visit to hell is not an ending event. You are stuck in hell if you do not come to Jesus. This ex-rich man would probably want to say be good, know God, worship God only, exalt his name. What was interesting is that this rich man wanted to warn his brothers. LUKE 16

HEAVENS GATE

2 Corinthians 9:8; And God is able to make all grace abound toward you, that you, always having all sufficiency in all things, may have abundance for every good work.

Sufficiency is telling us that we have enough to last and sustain us forever in Jesus Christ. The abundance means that we have plenty now and on the way. The Lord can do anything at anytime because time responds to him. He controls the future. He is able to make you and me rich at any given day. As a matter of fact all the people that are rich, He allowed them riches. The word clearly speaks of abundance. Now please understand that God uses the word abundance in the form of prosperity. It means blessings in all areas of your life. This abundance is not limited in blessings. God gives abundance in your life complete, your soul, spirit, mind, heart desire, prayer request, finances and you name it. As long as it is according to God' word and His will, it is abundance. Too often people limit God. These people have no control of God. He made the riches, silver, gold, homes and cars. Proverbs 10:22 The blessing of the Lord makes one rich, And He adds know sorrow with it.

Do you remember Jabez? O' that you might Bless Me! Many people think of that wonderful story of Jabez.
A familiar request came from Jabez, known as the prayer of Jabez. It speaks enlarge my territory. Bless me Lord. Enlarge and increase my territory. He said O that He might bless me. Many people have not understood that God has already increased and enlarged all the territory He desires for us. His blessings are so infinite. You can start counting but I guarantee you one thing for sure you will lose count.

Chronicle 8: 1-10 the prayer of Jabez is still alive. It is still in effect in our lives. There are many people who desire territory. Ask God to increase your territory. Bless me my Lord as long as I am obedient to you.

Jerimiah 33:3 Call to Me, and I will answer you, and show you great and mighty things, which you do not know.

God always answers. He said to call on Him and He will answer. He cannot lie. All truth is in Him. Malachi 3:1-10, Luke 6:38, Mark 10:

God is the potter and we are the clay. Please understand who made all things possible for all people.

Mark 10:21 Then Jesus, looking at him, loved him, and said to him, One thing you lack: Go your way, sell whatever you have and give to the poor, and you will have treasure in heaven; and come, take up the cross and follow Me.

CHAPTER 9

TAKE GODLY STEPS- STEP OUT

Exodus 8

REVERSE THE TIDE: Take Godly steps to serve God and be in step with Him when He calls on you for a new assignment. Reverse the old you and ask God what you will have me to do in service. Godly steps require obedience.

Moses is historically known to take Godly steps when he stepped into Egypt and confronted Pharaoh with instructions from God. In *Exodus 8:1 "And the LORD spake unto Moses, Go unto Pharaoh, and say unto him, Thus saith the LORD, Let my people go, that they may serve me."* It is not difficult to overcome doubt and confusion about your walk with Him. God gives the assignment and we must obey Him to please Him. Begin in prayer and know that you are talking to the most powerful person that lives, God the Father. Most people that are still blinded by something still have questions about how to walk with Him. You quickly turn to the disciples who walk with Him during His ministry on earth. They walk and they learned about the ministry and the church and key points about life such as obedience, faith, love, healing and trusting Him. They learned about the fruit of the Spirit. The attitude all Christians must have.

Have you ever considered walking in your blessings before? What are some of the blessings you would like to walk in? You can walk in your ministry calling. It is the power of God who gives such gifts to walk in those callings. You can walk in the power of deliverance ministry. Many people are missing that kind of ministry. You can walk like men of faith God describes in Hebrews 11. You may not walk exactly like them. But the same God still lives and He will direct your path according to His purpose. I know many people get confused about spiritual blessing and natural blessings. But God is the giver of both. So then if someone wants to bless you with one million dollars or more you can accept the gift and walk in it. After all there is abundance in millions. There is abundance in billions. You can become a millionaire and still acknowledge that God blessed you and then turn around and bless someone else.

Our faith walk is a blessing because it allows us to walk by faith and not by sight through the power of the Holy Spirit 2 Corinthians 5:7. We also walk to please God in our faith walk. Jesus is the only one who enters your body to make the change. The Holy Spirit works on us daily. I believe anyone who has an anointing on their lives can walk with Him. I must remind you of the horrible story that happen with a man in the bible. He was possessed with many legions of demons. Until one day he met Jesus and Jesus called the demons out of the man and sent them freely into the swine, which went into the water.

Genesis 5:24 tells us that Enoch walked with God. Moses said, *So all the days of Enoch walked with God; and he was not, for God took him.*

What an opportunity to be so blessed that He actually walked with God. Enoch was 365 years old and walked with God each year. What great endurance and sacrifice of time. One blessing here is the obedience to walk with God each year regardless of the trials and hardship. God rewards us with blessings when we are obedient to Him.

God never stop His blessings Psalms 23:4, David said, Yea, though I walk through the valley of the shadow of death, I will fear know evil; for you are with me; your rod and your staff they comfort me."

Every time we find ourselves in valley situation in which we do not understand or we find ourselves helpless, we have a Shepherd who leads us through our own personal valley. The blessing is that God is with you in your valley experience. Some of the worst moments in our lives God is right there in the valley waiting with open arms to catch us. David reminds us that God is the God of compassion and deliverance. David signifies that the rod and staff is a power source from God to comfort us just as He used Moses to comfort the Israelites while being emancipated and delivered from Egypt by Moses with the power of God in Him. His rod represents God's power. Moses helped God's people walk out of Egypt with their heads up and with dignity and honor. That is an awesome display of God's sovereignty. Only the hand of God could remove such evil to set people free. Only God could give people an attitude of dignity and honor. In our lives God wants us to be free to recognize what He alone has done for us. God will walk through the valley with you and bring you close to Him. I thank God that Israel was able to walk through the valley. The desert at times was the valley. At a moment in time the valley was the red sea. The children of Israel did not know how they were going to get through with Pharaoh on the chase. They were able to walk through the red sea. They were able to walk in the desert for forty years. God always has a blessing stored up. God always display His blessings that man is not equipped to take away. God has blessings planned for you. We all should walk with God.

In Galatians 5:16, we are told to *Walk in the Spirit, and you shall not for fill the lust of the flesh.* For the flesh lusts against the Spirit, and the Spirit against the flesh; and theses are contrary to one another, so that you do not do the things that you wish. But if you are led by the Spirit, you are not under the law. The blessing is that you are under God's control when you walk in the Spirit. The Holy Spirit leads people because they have submitted to Him Jesus as Lord and Redeemer. So then because you have made this decision in your life, you can be confident that Christ Jesus will do a new work in your life. You can be confident that Jesus knows you by name and is watching your service for His Kingdom. In fact, He is guiding you in His love. In Regina's case she still has the power to walk in Spirit. She is experiencing the age old manipulation by the enemy called sin stain. This is when the deceives on the sneak. He poisons little by little with the things like jealousy that sin that seem not so important but can lead to a bad position in life. Regina has to develop a new attitude of knowing who your redeemer is and where your blessings come from.

She will realize that her walk is with the Son of God, Jesus Christ. She is an over comer of sin and has a new walk today.

BLESSED THROUGH SIN STAIN

Do not allow sin stains to destroy your life. God has an awakening for you. I will start my physical exercise, walks and run as usual. It is just that Romeo keeps following me around to interrupting my glow. High Honey, This is the time to see the boss.

CHAPTER 10

GET BAPTIZED

ACTS 2:3-4; MATTHEW 28

REVERSE: RECEIVE BLESSINGS, BE OBEDIENT AND BE BAPTIZED IN
THE NAME OF THE FATHER SON AND HOLY SPIRIT.

In our society orders and commands are directed from the highest position, The Commander in Chief to his top general of the war ordering his subordinate commanders to execute multiple missions that require the best of strategic warfare planning and execution possible. It would be synchronized, battle planned, rehearsed and well executed. Orders are given and men follow those orders. If orders are not followed men die and injuries occur.

During my career, I have been questioned over and over by high ranking authorities that I believe are brilliant in military strategy, leadership and directly managing missions to see them all the way through. At a conference, I met an officer who had questions about baptism. My answer to him was that baptism represents the resurrection of Jesus out of the grave as he was laid down with a body that too all sin, but he was raise with all power and sin was destroyed. Baptism is symbolic of Jesus rising up from the dead and it is a sign of your individual obedience to his word in Matthew 28. So Baptism does count because Jesus wants us to be baptized. Similar to the orders and commands on the battle field, God commands us to get baptized. God made it possible for us to experience the blessedness of Baptism. The bible says there is only one baptism. When Jesus came to the Jordan He told John to suffer it must be that we fulfill this thing. To illustrate the point of importance of Baptism to God, he sent His son to get baptized as well. Jesus went into the water immersed and rose from the water as from a grave. When he rose from the water, He was showing us the significance of rising from the grave as well. Jesus' baptism shows us the agreement of the Father, Son and Holy Spirit by the evidence seen and heard. That particular time God's spirit rested on Jesus from Heaven as a dove. Then He said this is my son in whom I am well pleased. We should want God to be pleased with us in all of what we do. I was baptized when I was a little boy and my mother took her three boys. Still to this day I believe momma knew something about the Lord's blessing. What a difference it makes when we can still remember such a special moment in our lives.

Matthew 28:18-20: Jesus was speaking to His disciples. And Jesus came and spoke to them saying, all authority has been given to me in heaven and on earth. Go therefore and make disciples of all the nations, baptizing them in the name of the Father and of the Son and of the Holy Spirit, teaching them to observe all things that I have commanded you; and lo I am with you always, even to the end of the age.

According to Dobson et al.,(1994) Baptizing the believers who has been converted is the first step of outward obedience to the Lord and brings entrance into a local church. (Dobson, et al.,1994 The Greek word for Baptism is baptizo which is a English transliteration which means to "dip" or "dunk" or "immerse" indicating the proper method. Jesus requires those born again to be immersed. Jesus was also immersed by John the Baptist in Mark 3. Jesus commanded the disciples to baptize new believers in the name of the Father, Son and Holy Spirit. What a blessing to know the power of the Trinity is in agreement with your baptism. It is a powerful thought to know that you symbolically rose with Jesus Christ from the grave into a new life (Dobson, et al.,1994) .

Romans 6:4 The Apostle Paul wrote therefore we were buried with Him through baptism into death, that just as Christ was raised from the dead by the glory of the Father, even so we also should walk in newness of life.

74

God wants us to be a witness to all people about Him. We get baptized to symbolically reveal the outward death and resurrection of Jesus. We show the world that we have an inward relationship while demonstrating obedience to Jesus. Baptism is the second step after accepting Jesus as personal savior. Accepting Jesus is the saving power because you ask Jesus to come in your heart. Baptism is an outward expression symbolizing the death and burial of Jesus Christ our Lord. We get baptized to under obedience and acknowledge that our old nature of sin has died and was buried and we walk in a new life with the power that raised Jesus from the dead. The new life is the blessing that God gives us. The blessing is Jesus' sacrifice on the cross and taking the sting out of death that we might live forever. John said that one would baptize with fire in Mark 3. Make no mistake that this chapter is pointing you to obedience that you would ask the Holy Spirit to baptize you in the spirit and you make a decision to get baptized in the water by the command of Jesus Christ to His disciples.

In Act 2:3-4, it says, "And suddenly there came a sound from heaven, as of a rushing mighty wind, and it filled the whole house where they were sitting. And they were all filled with the Holy Spirit and began to speak with other tongues, as the Spirit gave them utterance."

The Holy Spirit fell on 120 believers on the day of Pentecost. Pentecost means fiftieth in Leviticus 23:16. Pentecost was represented by the feast of the weeks in Exodus 34:22. It was known to be seven weeks or 50 days after the start of barely harvest in Deuteronomy 16:10. Pentecost is known to represent radical ministry for the church because you are filled in the spirit. Pentecost represents 50 days after the Sabbath of Passover week.

The infilling of the Holy Spirit will empower you in your life to witness on earth. When you get baptized in the Holy Spirit, your life will forever change. When you are baptized in the Holy Spirit, you get empowered by God and the Lord uses you for a witnessing tool to people everywhere you go. When you are baptized in the Holy Spirit, you will no longer be ashamed of the Gospel. You will spread the Good News, the Word of God. The baptism of the Holy Spirit makes you an empowered person. You become a witness for Jesus Christ, telling everyone about the name and power of Jesus Christ. Get to a place and ask the Holy Spirit to fill your heart. The Lord indicated that those who were filled with the Holy Spirit spoke in tongues on that day. Speaking in tongues is a specific language communicating to God. It is a precious and holy language that connects us to God. This scripture is written for encouragement to be filled with the Holy Ghost and speak in tongues. The reason people debate speaking in tongues is because they are not thinking of the power that is in it and the devil blocks man's thinking with confusion. God is not a god of confusion. God is the God of truth, freedom and righteousness.

Get to a place and mediate and ask God to fill you with the Holy Ghost today. Be empowered to witness and use gifts that God gave you in the spirit. 1 Corinthians 12 and 14. See also Ephesians 4:11 for gifts.

CHAPTER 11

THE CROSS - CHANGED LIFE

God wants us to recognize the crucifixion

John 19

REVERSE: THE POWER OF SIN WAS BROKEN ON THE CROSS IN JESUS' BODY. HUMANITY WAS REVERSED. JESUS SAVED US. WE WERE RESCUED AND CHANGED, THEN GIVEN A SECOND CHANCE TO RECEIVE EVERLASTING LIFE AND HOPE.

Pinned down with all the emotional drama and intimidation at school is enough to drive anyone crazy. Fights were not fair where I grew up. If the enemy wanted to they could hold you down. That is exactly what happened to Alexander Payne. A lot of big kids ganged up on him and tackled him to the ground. Once they knocked him down, five others pinned him with their weight on top. Bully season seems like it never ends. Every year hear comes Mr. Bully. What he does not know is that he is really not the toughest or fearful person on the block or in school. The one that he keeps on messing with is the one that will turn things around for good. Obviously report it to the principle and teachers so they can call the police. The bully has to be put in check. The bully reminds me of the devil attacks. I must say also first of all it should be a shame to have a child that is a bully. Much like the human bully, the devil waits around the corner to attack you and to make you have a bad day. He attacks in the spirit realm to bruise your spirit man with the effort to destroy it. If it were left up to the devil, he would take your life. However, it is not up to that evil one. God is still in control and he will not let go of your life. We have an advocate on our side, Jesus Christ. Jesus gave the evil one a black eye and defeated him in all ways, nothing left undone. The next time you see a bully, give him your bag lunch and say hey you can have this. It is when he looks inside and sees that scripture on top of those cookies in the bag and read just one word, it then when his life is changed from bully to helper of the ministry of Jesus Christ. Your bully will come to Christ and become a protector for you and runner for the Lord Himself.

Jesus Christ broke the power of sin on the cross with His death. He took on every sin in humanity. Why worry about anything else on earth. The problem with worrying about other things is man's natural man constantly processes it and works against the work of the Spirit. When we consider the reality of the cross, we can easily identify the old wretched man that continually puts forth the effort to press temptation of sin again and again. One of the best solutions is to carry your cross so you can be constantly reminded of the power of love that took us through that ugly state of sin. You can remember how He brought you through the sin desire that once bound you and me on a daily basis. That is why my decision today is to meditate in worship and praise to Jesus remembering the crucifixion of Jesus. I believe in the sanctified imagination that we will walk in blessings all the days of our lives because of Jesus. When you consider the power of walking in blessing, consider that sin no has no authority over you. You are brand new in the sight of God because you have accepted the son of God, Jesus. No more broken life. No more out of God's blessed will. No more searching to fill the empty void. Jesus has broken the gates of sin and restored you again from all iniquity in your life. He has set us free. Yes, free indeed. *John 19:25 Now there stood by the cross of Jesus His mother, and His mother's sister, Mary, the wife of Clopas, and Mary Magdalene.*

John 19:28-30 after this Jesus knowing that all things were now accomplished; that the Scripture might be fulfilled said I thirst. Now a vessel full of sour wine was sitting there; and they filled a sponge with sour wine, put it on hyssop, and put it to His mouth. So when Jesus had received the sour wine, he said, "It is finished!"

ANCHORED TO RESSURRECTION:

Mark 16: 5-6 entering the tomb, they saw a young man clothed in a long white robe sitting on the right side; and they were alarmed. But he said to them, do not be alarmed. You seek Jesus of Nazareth, who was crucified. He has risen! He is not here. See the place where they laid Him.

Colossians 1:18-20. And He is the head of the body, the church, which is the beginning, the firstborn from the dead, that in all things He may have the preeminence. For it pleased the Father that in Him all the fullness should dwell, and by Him to reconcile all things to Himself, by Him whether things on earth or things in heaven, having made peace through the blood of His cross.

There could be no other possible way of expressing the truth in this story but that the love of God, which is shed abroad, is responsible for such an act. Jesus knew what was going to happen all along. He wanted His disciples to understand. On one occasion, Jesus had to rebuke Peter because to speak that I will not be so was to insult God. God has always been a God of sacrifice. That is just what He did. He humbled himself to be a lamb slaughtered.

CHAPTER 12

THE PRIEST'S HOUSE

Hebrews 3, Ephesians 5

REVERSE: THE PRIEST BARE RESPONSIBLITIES OF HIS HOUSE. HIS AUTHORITY REVERSES ALL ATTACKS IN HIS HOUSE. HE MUST ALLOW JESUS THE HIGH PRIEST TO BE OVER HIS ENTIRE HOUSE FIRST. HE MAKES INTERCESSORY PRAYER ON MY BEHALF. PRIEST NEED TO PRAY IN AND OVER YOUR HOUSE. AND REVERS SITUATIONS

Hebrews 3:1-4 Therefore, holy brethren, partakers of the heavenly calling, consider the Apostle and High Priest of our confession, Christ Jesus, who was faithful to Him who appointed Him, as Moses also was faithful in all His house. For this one has been counted worthy of more glory than Moses, in as much as He who built the house has more honor than the house. For every house is built by someone, but He who built all things, is God.

Jesus was appointed by God and made Apostle and the High Priest that we make our confession to. Jesus is referred to as Apostle and High Priest to reflect His superior ministry. The writer point is to elevate Jesus with these words by saying that Jesus was sent directly by God. When the author mentions High Priest, He is referring to Jesus as mans direct intercessor to God. Jesus is revealed as faithful to the Father who appointed Him but even higher because of His position by His Father. He is announced as worthy of glory and more than Moses and anyone else ever. The keeper of your household has this authority. God is the builder and keeper of your house. Your household is supposed to be anchored right now in Christ Jesus. He is the builder of your house. He is the architect and designer of your house. Do not allow anything to flood your house. Do not allow anything to rip your house apart. You are a spiritual Man of God. You are spiritual woman of God. Stand on the solid rock.

There is a story in *Matthew 7:24-25 where Jesus was teaching how to build on a solid foundation. He said in this scenario "Anyone who listens to the teaching and follows it is wise, like a person who build his house on a solid rock. Though the rain comes in torrents and the flood waters rise and wind beats against the house, it won't collapse because it is built on bedrock."*

Jesus must be the priest of your house because you as the man of the house need a foundation as priest. The man of the house needs a covering over himself and his family. You need to report to someone everyday to keep you on the right path and to live Holy. The Lord our God is the one who build your house. Give him glory and credit for everything! You must be humble priest to connect with God and get results and blessings. You need to connect with God because you are responsible and accountable for your house. You must become a praying priest. You are a praying priest because the enemy sees you and I like prey. He desires to chase us in our homes, at work and at church. The next time you have a serious disturbance in one of those locations or anywhere, it is because the enemy is mad at your position and your prayers. You must seek God and be faithful to Him. It is the Lord who will help you connect to the heavenly callings of your life.

THE PRIEST IN HIS HOUSE.

In the Priest House life takes on a new meaning. Nothing can stop the priest from communing with God. When the Priest is in the house, the house is covered and those inside the Priest house. Jack wants everyone to know that he is the head of the house, the priest of the house. There are commitments to being a priest in your house and God's house.

This priest in the house must be capable of responding to God in order to anchor the house. No one wants a lose house that anything can enter and destroy that house. It takes someone with the authority of God in his heart. It takes someone who has a relationship with the Lord. He needs to seek God and hear God speaking to him daily. Then he needs to speak to the Lord in prayer and in praise. He must be a responsible priest of the Lord for his house. The priest must know that he is the priest under the power and authority of the Lord. Since so many men are married and seeking to build the right and necessary house for his wife, it would be spiritually beneficial to be converted and know God for himself. Your house depends on you and the fact that you can lead them and make the best decisions for the family's spiritual growth. The wife looks for her husband's conversion because it comforts her to know that she has a God appointed man over her life. The only way the man can take a stand to make this happen is by simply saying to God; Lord, come into my heart and change me today. Help me to lead my family as a man of God. I believe that you are the son of God. I believe that you died and rose from the dead. I believe that God raised you from the grave and gave you all power and authority. I repent of my sin. Thank you for coming into my heart. Now make me the priest and man of my house. No man can be a true priest of his house unless he accepts Jesus Christ as Savior. Why would any man not want to accept Jesus as Lord in his life? Jesus accepts us each day regardless of our circumstances. Your house is anchored by the authority inside of your house.

Ephesians 5:25-27 Husbands, love your wives, just as Christ loved the church and gave Himself for her, that He might sanctify and cleanse her with the washing of water by the word. That He might present her to Himself a glorious church, not having spot or wrinkle or any such thing, but that she should be holy and without blemish.

God blessed Adam with all dominion. He blessed Adam to be in charge of all kingdoms on Earth as His agent. God controls all kingdoms. He blessed Adam with a wife. He blessed everyman who chose a wife and told us that she needed to be loved. So really Adam could do nothing without God. He blessed Adam to be the head of the house. Adam was provided with a garden that represented paradise, heaven itself. Because He blessed Adam He really blessed all descendants from Adam. Adam was an extension of God on earth blessing creation through the power of God. As a result of Adam, our Lord blessed all men. Do not misunderstand the fact that sin entered the world as a result of both Adam and Eve. Eve was lowered into deception by the serpent. But make no mistake about it, Adam had all dominion and all rule under the authority of God. So he was capable of blessing her and telling the enemy to go back to hell. Adam just like men today failed to call on the Lord even in that time of temptation and deception. It stems from Adam, the first man that we are able to choose either blessings or cursing. We were made to choose blessings over cursing regardless of the trickery and evil deeds of the enemy. Adam was blessed even in the midst of trouble. Adam was blessed although the enemy had tricked Him. The point here is that God never stops his blessings. Nothing can separate us from His blessings. Surely His blesses us because of His love for us. He also wants His men to be the priest of the house and lead the family.

David reminds us in *Psalm 1:1-2. Blessed is the man, who walks not in the counsel of the ungodly, Nor stand in the path of the sinner, nor sit in the seat of the scornful. For His delight is in the law of the Lord.* God desires that all His men be blessed no matter what the situation may look like. You are still blessed. Every man must get in the habit of delighting himself in the Lord and meditating on the Lord day and night. This delight is not you exalting yourself but it is exalting the savior. This delight is what God wants. It is a humble and obedient spirited man. God wants a man or woman who will bow down at the thought of His goodness. He wants men who will not live by the counsel or rule that is outside of His law. It is interesting because God is looking for men like Moses, Joshua, Abraham, Jacob, David, and Joseph. He is looking for men who will walk in His statutes and law. Most men when they really understand who God is will walk with God. Their delight will be in God. The thought of God will remain on the mind of a good man. Every man needs God in his life to be a Godly husband. He needs God because the Lord will help him to become the best husband he can possibly be.

One of the most interesting blessings that God has given to man is the order of priesthood. Man is by order the priest of the House. That is an inherited blessing from the Lord. His wife looks for that when she looks at him. She was never aware fully of what she expected but it was already placed inside of her to expect what He has from God. God conditioned her to expect him to be a priest. Now when sin raised its ugly head against Eve, God already knew. She took her eyes off of the order of her God and her husband and lost sight of his position. That is one of the leading problems in the home today. You see the priest of the house, the husband is the priest because he must walk in the counsel of God and meditate on him day and night. He is the priest because he must provide protections for his house. God wants every man to claim his position as a Priest over his family and home in Jesus Christ our Lord. So you can walk in the counsel of God and not the counsel of ungodly. That is the man who is blessed. His life is filled in Christ Jesus. That man takes his role serious in walking, fellowship, prayer, and spending time with God. The Lord helps us to spend the quality time that the wife and the family expect of us as well as God expect of us. A blessed man will focus on the family because he respects God word and reverences His order with the family.

Jeremiah 17:7-8 blessed is the man who trusts is in the Lord, And whose hope is the LORD. For he shall be like a tree planted by the waters , Which spread out its roots by the river, And will not fear when heat comes; But its leaf will be green, And will not be anxious in the year of drought, Nor will cease from yielding fruit.

The Lord blesses us when we trust Him. He wants us to maintain a trust in Him so He can keep on blessing us. Something that seems so simple yet is found so difficult to so many people. Nevertheless, when we realize that God wants us to be like that tree planted by the waters that keeps on receiving nourishment that enables him to be stronger revealing life's newness, we must keep on pressing in life. Their trust will help to fight off attacks while blessings are being granted.

84

Psalms 37:23 the steps of a good man are ordered by the Lord, and He delights in his way. Though he fall, he shall not be utterly cast down; For the Lord upholds him with His hand. I have been young and now old; yet have I not seen the righteous forsaken, Nor his descendants begging bread. He is ever merciful, and lends; and his descendants are blessed.

It is important for wives to see the power that exist in her husband. She must understand that God equips good men. So if her husband is a good man his steps are ordered by the Lord. We must acknowledge it. The man must understand that this good man David is talking about is a man who delights in God almighty.

CHAPTER 13

THE WOMAN I WANT TO BLESS

Ephesians 5

Ephesian 5: 22-27 Wives, submit yourselves unto your own husbands, as unto the Lord. For the husband is the head of the wife, even as Christ is the head of the church: and he is the savior of the body. Therefore as the church is subject unto Christ, so let the wives be to their own husbands in every thing. Husbands, love your wives, even as Christ also loved the church, and gave himself for it; That he might sanctify and cleanse it with the washing of water by the word, That he might present it to himself a glorious church, not having spot, or wrinkle, or any such thing; but that it should be holy and without blemish.

BLESS YOUR WIFE, BLESS YOUR HUSBAND

Reverse the Tide: Take on this new attitude with your loved one: I want to bless my wife. I want to bless my husband. I will present him or her with nothing less than the best.

God has truly blessed women. In accordance with Ephesians 5, the woman I want to bless is my wife. Thank God that He blessed my mother to give me this kind of mind and respect for a woman. My wife is a helper for me, her husband, she gives birth to children and insults Satan directly in his face and blesses the Lord almighty with the fruit of her womb. She gives Him thanks with sensitivity and worship recognized by God in her truest worship and praise stance. She knows how to open her heart to God. She knows the power of prayer and seeks God for her family. She is the desire that man wants in his life to be a soul mate on the winning team of the Alpha and the Omega, the beginning and the end. The Lord bases their relationship off the marriage vows and the commitment made before Him because they are solemn and holy in His sight. Get your wife and ask the Lord to bless her that your service and ministry will be to the glory of God.

He blessed her with life in the beginning when he created her. He blessed her in matrimony from the beginning of time. He revealed to her by His spirit what submission was all about. One of her first acts was submission. She submitted to God after she was formed from the rib He took from Adam's side. She submitted when God presented her to Adam. So it was not that Eve could not submit. She had the power and she did it. We know that she submitted to what the enticing enemy wanted her to do. But I believe God does not want women today to think on that situation but to think today that you have the power to God and your husband. God does not stop there. Because women's lives are surrounded by the special power of submission, she submits to her children and her entire family. She submits to her daily acts of love in her family. God has blessed wives so much that men sometimes miss her tenderness and her love. God designed her so unique it is mind boggling. She is the other half of the man. God calls her the helpmate. She helps him to stand. We often discuss the ribs meaning in Genesis. She is the support to him and structure to him. She is his greatest hero. The wife is the fruit bearer for God. She submits to bear fruit for God. She submits to bear fruit for her husband. The seed he supplies by God she brings forth the life from it. The woman is highly blessed. I am reminded of Mary, the mother of Jesus in whom the Angel said you are highly favored. She was highly favored because God recognized a woman with a good heart and a submissive relationship. God sees the woman who wants to be married. I believe every woman should be married to God first. Then you know she is a holy woman who adores God. God reminds us in a few scriptures below of the woman commitment.

Corinthians 7:3-5: Let the husband render to his wife the affection due her, and likewise also the wife to her husband. The wife does not have authority over her own body, but the husband does, And likewise the husband does not have authority over his own body, but the wife does.

Proverbs 31:10 who can find a virtuous wife? For her worth is far above rubies. The heart of her husband safely trusts her; so he will have no lack of gain. She does him good and not evil all the days of her life.

God blessed Sarah when she was barren, unable to have a child. Abraham and Sarah waited many years before God would allow them to have the promise child of their own. Abraham and Sarah asked constantly for this child and God heard them. He already had the blessing in Abraham's seed even when there was doubt. When Sarah allowed Abraham to go into Hagar to conceive an heir it seems as though she was taking it upon herself to satisfy her emptiness and void in her life. In today's society, that would not be the order. Women would not offer up their maids. I believe one point is the fact that when God put two people together He did not mean for it to be a third party. Jesus said that the two shall become one. So we see why God was displeased with Ishmael. He was not the promised child and not ordered by God. Yet the awesome God we know blessed Him. Ishmael was connected to a blessed man and woman.

God blessed Hanna because she trusted in Him in her prayers for a child. She could not have any children because as the Bible describes, her wound was dead. But God can do anything. She believed in God and He allowed her to bare a child.

Our father so rich in mercy helps relationships. He works on marriages that are remarkable today. Hosea and Gomer is one of the stories in the scripture that reflects how God helps in love relationship. They were married and she played the harlot and had children and this man Hosea remained faithful to God. I remember waiting on the repair man on a military base. When he came in to repair fixtures and electrical items, I thought I had a chance to witness. I struck up a conversation and then tailored it toward well the highest God. I told him that I was a minister. He responded to me that he was a pastor over a church and that was some years ago. I hesitated before my lips moved he stated his wife ran away with another man so he quit. That simple statement made me realize that life can deal you a blow and you can also let it deal you an extensive blow. He reminded me in that story to this day that I must be about my father's business and not be in this for any other reason. If I hold on to people to sustain me in the living God, then I fall. So I must trust Him as thought I am married to Him. God gives us a good wife, but men must teach his family about the family affairs and about the respect, honor, and glory to God our father.

God blessed Esther, who met a king and fell in love and at the same time protected her nation. She was highly favored and blessed by God and the King recognized it. So did the people around her. Esther had won the heart of the King and the nation. But more importantly, she was obedient, submissive and was pleasing in the sight of God. Throughout her time she carried herself like a woman of God and a queen. The king was pleased to have such a woman who touched his heart and his life. God will always send that special person in your life to help shape circumstances for the good and for His glory. A man wants a wife that he can depend on and relate to in the right spiritual mind and connection. The King needed someone to help guide him in his feelings so he could connect with the true King, our Lord. You can always be a good wife but if you want to better yourself for your family and your husband try hearing and following God. There is a difference in our lives when we hear from God rather than hearing from our own conscience. God will take you places that no one on earth can take you. He can take you places that we are unable to take ourselves. That is something to shout about! What a mighty God we have and mighty God we serve.

A FIRED UP AND BLESSED WIFE

More challenges in Jack household. The marriage anniversary role around and Jack forgot to send the roses to the office. Regina's friends knew all about the anniversary date. All of her friends were waiting with her to get those flowers, and see what jack was sending. They knew some other stuff too that Jack kept getting attacked by. The flowers did not come that day at the office because Jack was too disturbed to deal with what was happening in the marriage. He felt like it was deteriorating right before his very eyes. All along he knew what was in his heart. He needed to tell Regina how he truly felt.

Jack told Regina that he felt that fire was out because of the fling she had. Jack said, you hurt my heart real bad. Regina said, you don't understand. I did not sleep with him. It was just one mistake, a kiss that I should have avoided. With boldness and tenacity, Regina told Jack that I am sorry for that mistake but you are my man, my husband and I aren't any fool to let you go. Regina said, "I love you Jack. You are my hero and my lover and my best friend. Help me to pray for our relationship. Today I promise that I will be the best wife I can for my husband. Forgive me and help us to start clean slate Lord Jesus."

Regina's marriage has experienced some ups and bumps and bruises for 20 years but they hung in there, they kept it working. Somewhere along the time an affair almost happened. It was an innocent kiss but nothing happened.

CHAPTER 14

TRAIN YOUR CHILD

Proverbs 22

Proverbs: 22:6 Train up a child in the way he should go, and when he is old he will not depart from it.

REVERSE; TRAIN YOUR CHILD AND INFLUENCE THEM TO CHANGE NEGATIVE BEHAVIOR TO POSITIVES.

Imagine a trained up child in the things of God. Start early training your child about moral and who God is. Only God can touch the mind of a young person and influence them tremendously and at the same time turn them around in their tracks and place them on the best path of life for success. The word can keep your child in his or her early stages of life, youthful year, and through high school and college. Start them with memory exercises when it comes to learning the Bible. Start them with meditating on the word as well. A trained up child in the things of God is similar to arming a highly trained soldier ready for combat. Children know more than many parents and other grown-ups give them credit for. Sure a large number do give them credit, however, we are faced with our built in protection chips and we maintain our selves in that mode of thinking. Home is training ground for the parents to teach prayer, faith, salvation, that there is one God, the word period. The more parents allow outside sources to raise their children, the stronger the chance is that they might sway to the left. You could easily lose that child. I am telling today that the word of God will grip your child's soul, spirit, mind and heart. Today purchase your child that brand new Bible and a book to supplement the Bible. They will be forever grateful to you as a parent.

Training up a child at home is most crucial. More importantly is training your child up in the fear of the Lord Jesus Christ. Every parent is responsible for instilling values, discipline, love and care into their children. What you teach must be an anchor from the Lord in their lives. Every parent and child should want all of these important points to be life-long lessons that serve as key parts of living the Christian life.

You can train a child day and night in the Lord but they need to want God. If they seem to not want God, they still have to follow the rules in the house. Yes, the training rules. There is a standard in the house. You need to know that God has blessed everyone in the house. Sometimes it's just that somebody in the house; the child is not recognizing his or her blessings. They need to know that they are blessed with parents that love and nurture them until the end. One example comes to mind. Mary stood at the cross when Jesus hung on it while he suffered. She watched the most agonizing moments of Jesus' crucifixion. The point is simple. Your father and mother watched some of your worst moments and saw you through it. Jesus gave them the strength to do it. It just like God saw Jesus, His only begotten son in the worst moments. He did separate for a moment to allow the sin to be destroyed in his body for the whole world. That was a temporary separation and they came back together.

Our children need to know sometimes we may need to separate so they can grow and learn about society. You can learn about life. Let Mother's skirt go, let Dad's coattail go. Get off of them and grow up. Learn about who God really is.

Training sometimes comes from just observing your parents. When parents do right the child will do right. You go to church the child will go to church. You sing praises to the Lord; the child will eventually sing praises to the Lord. You worship the God of Abraham, Isaac, and Jacob. The Father of Jesus Christ our Lord, the child follows suit in worship, you study the Word of God, and the child studies the Word of God. There is a connection. Yes, the Father's influence and mother influence and nurturing gift of the mother all have impacts and the power to persuade our children. *Matthew 18:10 Despise not one of these little ones; for I say unto you that in heaven their angels do always behold the face of my father.*

Do not provoke the child to wrath. It seems in our lives that things can be at a standstill.

One of the primary characteristics that everyone should have is respect. Children must really understand the importance of respect perhaps before anything else. Respect is two ways with Parents and children as wells as friends. This type of respect lines up with knowing God. It is important that parents explain to children that you have respect first because your creator God, the Father designed each of us to respects one another. You will have much difficulty trying to respect someone without the Holy Spirit. You see if they do not have respect, they will not honor God. If Children do not honor God, they will not honor parents. Children need to respect God and their parents and people in general. When the scripture says train up a child, He is speaking of a reverence and obedient type of training. To reverence someone means to have the utmost respect and honor. This is a bow down type of honor. When you hear God's name mentioned you want to bow down. When you hear of God, your entire conscience goes into a state of worship and praise. It might be a silent praise and worship but you are moved at the very thought of who He is and what He has done. This reverence will give you a joy that you will respect God. Our children need to see that and let it stay on their minds, let it be etched in their minds and hearts to remember what you saw the father and the mother do in honoring God. We can be encouraged that God will work it out.

Training a child means help him or her avoid the pot holes of life or falling into the pits of hell. It takes a concentrated training effort to help your training. Neglect will surely push them into the pits of hell. We need to understand that many children do not believe mom and dad are up to date on things. When we help them, it does not mean they will be perfect children. It s not mean they will not make their own choices. It does not mean that they will not make mistakes. Many children end up homeless, in jail, in prison, lost, fatherless, and many other situations, but it does not mean that the training did not work. The word says my word will not go out and return void. David said, you word I hid in my heart that I may not sin against you. The word will work if you use it the greatest gift you can give your child is love. The love of God is the greatest gift. If directing them to God is your priority then give them the word. More word, more healing, more word, more worship, more word more thanksgiving. More word, more mountains moved by God. More word, more love shining forth by God through all of us. God wants us to speak the word of training a child. Once they get the word inside of them, they will stay with that word and start obeying God sometime in their life. Just watch God do the work in them.

Deuteronomy 6:3 Therefore hear, O Israel, and be careful to observe it, that it may be well with you, and that you may multiply greatly as the Lord God of your fathers has promised you-a Land flowing with milk and honey.

2 Timothy 1:5 When I call to remembrance the genuine faith that is in you, which dwelt first in your grandmother Lois and your mother Eunice, and I am persuaded is in you also.

2 Timothy 1:7 For God hath not given us the spirit of fear; but of power, and of love and of a
sound mind.

A Discerning Spirit is what all of God's children need. We need it to be leaders and followers in the faith of our Lord Jesus Christ. A Discerning spirit enables God's people to pick up on things that are not good and things that are evil. The Holy Spirit helps with understanding those things.   This is exactly what King Solomon was asking God for to lead his people. *1 King 3:7-9 O' Lord my God, you have made your servant king in places of my father David, But I am only a little child and do not know how to carry out my duties. Your servant is here among the people you have chosen, a great people, too numerous to count or number. So give your servant a discerning heart to govern your people and to distinguish between right and wrong. For who is able to govern this great people of yours?*

94

There were many good parents in the home according to the scripture. David trained up his son Solomon in the admonition of the Lord. God saw it and was pleased. There were many blessing that would result from that through training up his son. Solomon knew his father was rich in the Lord our God. He knew no man could be in a position like his father and be so humble before God almighty. It is so important that we set the example in the home first. God had everything planned out but He still wants the father to be the image setter. God blessed Solomon through David His servant. God made Solomon the most powerful man on earth at one time. God also gave him a blessing that know other man could go beyond of course other than Jesus. That was the blessing of a discerning heart, the power of wisdom and discernment to identify good and evil and make decision for God's people. Listen to what Solomon asked of the Lord: 1 Kings 3:7-9.

God's Blessing on Solomon's Life:

I KINGS 3:10-14 The Lord was pleased that Solomon had asked for this. So God said to him, since you have asked for this and not for long life or wealth for yourself, nor have asked for the death of your enemies but for discernment in administering justice, I will do what you have asked. I will give you a wise and discerning heart, so that there will never have been anyone like you, nor will there ever be.

Only God can blessed a man such to make him original. Only God can make a man's request be truly for filled. It is good to know that God's blessings on a man's child continues through his seed and passes through generations to come. All God asked is to train them up in the Lord.

God granting Solomon's request has to be one of the greatest moments in his life. God gave him such a blessing so he could deal with the precious lives of so many people. Discernment is the ability to see through things right or wrong, the ability to recognize the true nature of things and distinguish one thing from another. In many ways, it said that Solomon foreshadowed the greater Son of David, Jesus Christ. In the scripture Matt 12:42, *The Queen of the South will rise at the judgment with this generation and condemn it; for she came from the ends of the earth to listen to Solomon's wisdom, now one greater than Solomon is here" We know that only Jesus, the coming Messiah would demonstrate more wisdom than Solomon. Why? It is because Jesus is the son of the Living God.*

Jacob and Joseph blessing,

In Genesis 48: 14-16 Then Israel stretched out his right hand and laid it on Ephraim's head, who was the younger, and his left hand on Manasseh's head, guiding his hands knowingly, for Manasseh was the firstborn. And he blessed Joseph, and said God before whom my father Abraham and Isaac walked, The Go who has fed me all my life long to this day, The Angel who has redeemed me from all evil, Bless the lads;

It is interesting that we speak of this type subject. God deals with so many cases in His word. In the life of Jacob, it was customary to bless the firstborn son. Jacob of course had twelve sons himself. His favorite son was Joseph. We know this to be true because the Bible tells us that Jacob made him a coat of many colors. This coat was designed specifically for Joseph to see that his father loved him so much and identified with his as a royal son. Sons are blessed abundantly even when they do not see it at the moment. Now listen to this. Joseph had two sons that were brought to Jacob before he was to die. On the death bed the grandfather of Ephraim and Manasseh was presented to Jacob so that Jacob would bless them. Joseph expected the first born to receive the right hand blessing from God but Jacob blessed the least likely son which was Ephraim.

Joseph's Brother Blessings, and Joseph's Cup,

In Genesis Chapter 44, the Lord God moves in Joseph's heart to make him love his brothers by not harboring any hate. Instead he blessed them. What an example of how blood brothers and even spiritual brothers should bless one another. The blessing is where all the good things dwell.

CHAPTER 15

A GOD CENTERED MARRIAGE

Genesis 2

BONE OF MY BONE, FLESH OF MY FLESH

Gen 2: 24 Therefore a man shall leave his father and mother and be joined to his wife, and they shall become one flesh.

REVERSE: GOD WANTS YOU TO HAVE A GOD CENTERED MARRIAGE. KEEP YOUR VOWS SACRED. IT INVOLVES LOVE KNOWING GOD AND LOVING ONE ANOTHER. LOVE IS THE FOUNDATION FOR A GOD CENTERED AND SUCCESSFUL MARRIAGE. IT CAN BE BLESSED BY GOD AND MAINTAINED BY HIM AS WELL IF YOU GET IN RELATIONSHIP BECAUSE YOU SHOULD BE EQUALLY YOKED .

Moses wrote this to represent the foundation and institution of marriage by God. God wants us to walk as one in marriage. Nothing divides you or comes between you. It is because your marriage is ordained by God. He knows already who you should marry and who you shouldn't. Make the best choice and do not settle for anything. Remember, your vows are sacred because you have done this in the eyes of God and with His blessings. Don't let anyone tear it apart. Seek God when trouble arises. Seek God everyday to change you and the situation. You might be the issue. The other person might be the issue and need help by prayer, listening and being understanding. Be real in your marriage. This is your marriage not your neighbors or best friend. Don't tell everything about your personal business to others but tell the Lord.

Mark 10: 6-9 But from the beginning of the creation, God made them male and female. For this reason a man shall leave his father and mother and be joined to his wife, and the two shall become one flesh so then they are no longer two but one flesh. Therefore what God has joined together, let not man separate.

BLESSING A SUBMISSIVE BRIDE

Ephesians 5 22-25: Wives, submit yourselves unto your own husbands, as unto the Lord. For the husband is the head of the wife, even as Christ is the head of the church: and he is the Savior of the body. Therefore as the church is subject unto Christ, so let the wives be to their own husband in everything. Husbands love your wives, even as Christ also loved the church, and gave himself for it.

The husband needs to know that he is the head of the marriage so be the head and take the family. When the wife knows that she can count on you and you are a loyal husband, she becomes a submissive bride. Wives you are to become submissive the night or day of the wedding. When you seal this marriage with the ring and intimacy, it was the first sign of being a submissive bride. The night of the wedding seals it all because of the level of intimacy. God takes your marriage seriously. Think about the night of intimacy after the wedding and how important it was to you. The reason why you are considered a bride is because there is a precious veil that covers your beauty that should never tarnish in the eyes of your husband. When he removes that veil, he then sees the gift that God had given him and is highly blessed and made to be one. She presents herself holy and all of her to her husband because she is now his wife. They are one. Everything Jesus did for us is to remind us that we are to be one with Him.

SUBMISSION IS POWERFUL

One of the common words in the passage above is submit. To have an attitude of submission is like having an attitude of obedience. We know the power of obedience because it wasn't until Adam and Eve got into a disobedient state of man that they acted it out. God seems to plan for the modeled couple to be submissive to one another. Throughout much scripture submission seems to be an act that gets God's attention. His twelve disciples submitted to Him. Most of us think of King David who wrote so many Psalms with a passion and a desire to know Him in His power. It is already ordained by God almighty. God is true to his word in marriage as he is with all areas of life. Marriage is perhaps the most exciting moment in life after accepting Jesus Christ in your heart. The Lord speaks about it as an institution. This is a commitment that is not to be taken lightly. When you marry someone you are one with that person. You grow over the years to become a better couple. When you stand before the priest to get married and make the commitment that day you have just entered into a covenant relationship with your spouse and more importantly with the Lord . You have just stood before the Lord while he is on His throne and in your presence and state that you take absolute full responsibility of your wife and to the wives, your husband. These scriptures below are written to anchor your marriage. God is forever looking down on those that call themselves children of God and those that are truly in sync with Him. God is looking for a bride for His return.

Someone asked the question about marriage. The question is and was why did I get married? Some people marry out of convenience. Some marry for multiple reasons. Some marry for love and some marry for security. The marriage everyone should seek first is the marriage with the Lord Jesus Christ. He will love you forever. God will keep you forever. When you need love that seems like you are lacking, God will love you then. When you seem like you need extra love, God will give you extra love. When love seems to be lost, God will supply more love. You see He has an unlimited supply of love. He will never run out. So the answer to why did I get married is simple. He will love me forever and ever with a real love than can never be exhausted. His love is unconditional love.

Colossians 3:18-19 Wives, submit to your own husbands, as is fitting in the Lord. Husbands love your wives and do not be bitter toward them.

Husbands, you are the priest of the house and wives you are the helpmeet to maintain the home. The husband is responsible for having a house in order and the wife stands by his side in all things before the lord. This is pleasing to the Lord. They agree that is why he made them two as one. A man and a woman have a special union that ties them together spiritually and intimately. It was designed to be a lasting relationship. Only a few species like the eagle live lasting relationships with their mate. Surely if an eagle can do it, humans can do it.

Corinthians 7:3 Let the husband render to his wife the affection due her, and likewise also the wife to her husband.

The husband is responsible for showing his wife love and affection as is the wife is responsible for demonstrating the love and affection to her husband. This love and affection is not an option. This affection is a requirement to keep you bonded as one. Remember, let no one divide you. You keep your relationship together by affection. This affection is love. Do not let anyone come into your marriage and tell you how to be married except the Holy Spirit. There can be some friendly advice but ultimately, it must be the Holy Spirit guiding you.

1 Peter 3:7 Husbands, likewise, sell with them with understanding, giving honor to the wife, as to the weaker vessel, and as being heirs together of the grace of life, that your prayers may not be hindered.

HOSEA AND GOMER

Hosea 1:2-9: the beginning of the word of the Lord by Hosea. And the Lord said to Hosea, Go take unto thee a wife of whoredoms and children of whoredoms; for the land hath committed great whoredom, departing from the Lord. So he went and took Gomer the daughter of Diblaim; who conceived, and bore him a son.

Our father so rich in mercy helps marriages and all relationships. He works on the marriages that are made remarkable today. God expects believers to be faithful to their vows and commitment to Him. We see God as the one who blesses the sanctity of marriage.

1 Peter 3: 8-12 Finally, be ye all of one mind, having compassion one of another, love as brethren, be pitiful, be courteous: Not rendering evil for evil, or railing for railing: but contrariwise blessing; knowing that ye are thereunto called, that ye should inherit a blessing. For he that will love life, and see good days, let him refrain his tongue from evil, and his lips that they speak no guile: Let him eschew evil, and do good; let him seek peace, and ensue it. For the eyes of the Lord are over the righteous, and his ears are open unto their prayers: but the face of the Lord is against them that do evil.

Mary was one of the most loyal women in the Bible.. She had a relationship with God which makes her so popular among everyone especially women. Her relationship was so close to God that He chose her to give birth to Jesus. Mary was a virgin and she kept herself for the Lord. Young ladies it okay to be a virgin until you are married. God will bless you. Don't worry about people saying anything. God will bless you.

Marital vows: They mean you are committed to that one person. It symbolizes a state of oneness.

Why go into a marriage? Love is the key ingredient and primary above all. Jesus must be center
How do you keep it strong? Love with the mind of Christ
Why is it necessary to be marriage?
Why remain marriage?

Here is one solution that all married person should think on:

Proverbs 5:15-18:
15 Drink water from your own cistern,
And running water from your own well.
16 Should your fountains be dispersed abroad?

Streams of water in the streets?
17 Let them be only your own,
and not for strangers with you.
18 Let your fountain be blessed,
And rejoice with the wife of your youth.

The woman is yours. You have no need to commit adultery and fornication. God gave you a wife as gift and she supplies all of what you desire and need on the intimate level. Solomon had issues with many women. He saw a woman and to him she belongs to him. Solomon had a thirst for multiple women.

CHAPTER 16

OVERCOMING YOUR IDENTITY CRISIS

Matthew 16

Matthew 16:16-19 When Jesus came into the region of Caesarea Philippi, He asked His disciples, saying Who do men say that I, the Son of Man, am? So they said, "Some say John the Baptist, some Elijah, and others Jeremiah or one of the prophets. "He said to them, "But who do you say that I am?" Simon Peter Answered and said, You are the Christ, the son of the living God. *Matthew 16:17-19 Jesus answered and said to him, "Blessed are you, Simon Bar-Jonah, for flesh and blood has not revealed this to you, but My Father who is in heaven. "And I also say to you that you are Peter, and on this rock I will build My church, and the gates of Hades shall not prevail against it. "And I will give you the keys to the kingdom of heaven, and whatever you bind on earth will be bound in heaven, and whatever you loose on earth will be loosed in heaven."*

REVERSE: GOD WANTS YOU TO KNOW YOUR IDENTITY. KNOW WHO YOU ARE! IF ANY DOUBT ASK GOD TO GUIDE YOU. OVERCOME YOUR CRISIS BY GIVING IT TO JESUS CHRIST. HE WILL HELP YOU MORE THAN ANYONE.

God speaks to Peter directly to let him know that he has an assignment for the Church. He let him know by identifying who he is now. You see the enemy wants the church just like he wanted heaven. The enemy is at the gates of hell but the gates of hell shall not prevail. Did you see that? God truly established His church and authority in one of His men. God did not want Peter to think that he could do it alone. So He has given Peter the necessary weapon to sustain the church.

God used the word Rock to express the foundation and the authority of His son, Jesus. Many of us express that word rock as someone we can rely on. Some see it as the one who is strong in the house, the one to lean on in times of crisis. When we were growing up, there was always someone in the house who was the rock. That person was the go to person. Any problems in your life or your marriage, finances, sickness, Aunt Betty had a solution for it. She knew how to comfort and persuade you that everything will be alright. Sometimes it would be another person, telling you that God will bless you.

Colossians 1:18-20: And he is the head of the body, the church, who is the beginning, the firstborn from the dead, that in all things he may have the preeminence. For it pleased the Father that in Him all the fullness should dwell: and by Him to reconcile all things to Himself, by Him, whether things on earth or things in heaven, having made peace through the blood of His cross.

We have been blessed exceedingly by our Lord Jesus Christ because it is in the church where we find sanctity, peace and harmony and an atmosphere of holiness that man struggles with comprehending the debts and realm of it. Jesus provides that dimension of our lives. The church is our place of worship. The church is our dwelling place with God. The church is our place where we find our high priest awaiting each Sunday and throughout the week. The church is God's temple. The church is Christ Jesus inside of us. We worship Him filled in His Holy Spirit as we walk about in our daily business.

Jesus established the church and Jesus is the head of the church. Jesus controls the church. Although His people makeup the body of the church, He alone controls the destiny of the church. The church is where true worshippers attend. The church is where the broken show up to get fixed and connect their lives with Jesus. The church is where the sick come for healing. The church is where relationships come to be restored. The church is where there are people that are scared but they come to request that their scars be removed. The church is a place of Holiness. God said without Holiness man will not see God. Once you get Jesus inside you, you are a Holy man or woman. Do not let anyone tell you different, you are holy through Christ Jesus. The church is where true worshipers go. The church is where men and women acknowledge Him as the Christ, the son of the living God.

104

Please do not mistake the inside of the temple or tabernacle where we worship as the only dwelling place or place of acknowledgment. We go to fellowship and worship in the spirit of Christ, Jesus. We attend because of His everlasting love and obedience to our savior as servants. He rules in the very heart of man and He blesses us beyond imagination.

Ephesians 4:11 tells about the blessings that God gave to the church. And He Himself gave some to be apostles, some prophets, some evangelists, some pastors and teachers, for the equipping of the saints for the work of ministry, for the edifying of the body of Christ.

When it seems like society has dealt a blow, even when it seems like everyone has cast you aside as though you are nothing, God our Lord shows Himself alive in your life each time. God, our Lord shows us what He gave to establish the Church, the one He is looking for without spot or wrinkle as the word says. He gave the fivefold ministry with power everlasting because He is everlasting. Our Lord equipped man through and by the living word of God and called them to be an apostle, prophet, evangelist, pastors, and teachers. The scripture continues and it says for the equipping of the saints for the work of the ministry, for the edifying of the body of Christ, till we all come to the unity of the faith and of the knowledge of the Son of God, to a perfect man, to the measure of stature of the fullness of Christ. God covers His ministries throughout the world with the power of His word. We can rest assured that because God established these ministries that man and no one in all creation could never can change what He has already destined and ordained. One of the most devastating events occurred in the world today was the misuse of the office and appointment in these ministries. The enemy has gone all out to attack the minds and flesh of men called Priest of the five-fold ministry. The church was faced with the ugliest sexual abuse scandal perhaps ever in the history of the church. We must understand the call to ministry and that it separates a man from the call of the enemy and flesh obsessions and uncontrollable desires. The encouraging point to this is that no matter how much the church will go through, God is always and will never leave us nor forsakes us. He will continue to bless those that are called according to His purpose. Jesus established it all and He will never let His anointed ones fall. He said in Jude 24-25 Now unto Him who is able to keep you from falling and to present you faultless before the present of His glory with exceeding joy. To the only wise God our Savoir, Be glory and majesty and dominion now and forever. Amen.

Have you ever been in a place and the atmosphere was sour and creepy and you felt that at any moment turmoil and the hood mentality would erupt in a moment's notice. The church is the opposite. You are in a place where in a moment's notice, the Holy Spirit can and will erupt and interrupt your planned of service and your schedule for that day. For the word says in John 3:8 The wind blows where wishes, and you hear the sound of it, but cannot tell where it comes from and where it goes so is everyone who is born of the Spirit. Now you might not be born of the Spirit but God in with fullness of His power will change you, your day and your circumstance.

Matthew 16: List the Keys

God is also looking for the Church to be without Spot or Wrinkle. He will come again and receive it to Himself. God has all rule and authority over all things. Seven keys God, our Lord is looking for in His Church that He established.

Key 1: Obedience to the call- You do what God asks of you. Do not hold back because God has ordained it.

Key 2: Humility-Not puffed up, but a mild humble and meek in spirit person.

Key 3: Five Fold Ministry- They are listed as those in Ephesians 4

Key 4 Son of God- Jesus Christ who was birthed by a virgin and sent by God

106

Key 5: The power to bless others- If you are a Christian you have the power to pass on blessings through Jesus Christ

Key 6: The love of God- John 3:16. You have to be ignoring God to miss this statement in the Bible.

Key 7: Sanctified with true holiness: The Holy Spirit is working on the believers heart so that He can work in the ministry.

Key 8: Gifts; See 1 Corinthians 12, 14, Ephesians 4. God gave gifts in the Spirit.

God also gives us another example of what the Church should be like, not dead. He uses *Ezekiel 37: 1-5 The Lord took hold of me, and I was carried away by the Spirit of the Lord to valley filled with bones. He led me all around among the bones that covered the valley for. They were scattered everywhere across the ground and were completely dried out. Then He asked me, Son of man, can these bones become living people again? O'Sovereign Lord, I replied, you alone know the answer to that. Then He said to me, Speak a prophetic message to these bones and say, Dry bones, Listen to the word of the Lord! This is what the Sovereign Lord says: Look! I am going to put breath into you and make you live again!*

God is speaking of resurrecting a church from its dead state to lively state. God wants church to be on fire for His Kingdom. One of things that stand out in my mind more and more each day is the ministry of the church. Where is the ministry supposed to operate? Well, in the scripture Jesus tells us to visit the poor, the prisons, the homeless, and those most unfortunate. The church is obligated to getting out of the walls to minister a strong ministry of need and hope to the helpless. Christians should do things similar to the feed the children ministry program. I believe there are so many organizations now but the emphasis is still lacking. Where organizations miss a beat the church should stand in the gap. Often I think of a new program of hope.

Chapter 2-6 of Revelation reveals seven seals of the Church

I believe it is vitality important to understand that God has a seal on the lives of His servants for the Church. Revelation reveals to us visual display of what God wants in the Church. We need to be clear upfront that God is looking for a Church without spot or wrinkle. In Revelation He speaks of the seven seals of the Church.

CHAPTER 17

REVERSE THE ENEMY'S FLOODS

Genesis 9

Gen 9: 1 So God blessed Noah and his sons, and said to them: be fruitful and multiply, and fill the earth.

REVERSE: GOD WANTS YOU TO FIGHT BACK AND REVERSE ALL OF THE ENEMY ATTACKS. DON'T BE LIKE THE PEOPLE THAT IGNORED NOAH WHEN GOD LEFT A WINDOW OF OPPORTUNITY TO BE SAVED. LISTEN TO GOD.

God holds back the flood gates and no demon in Hell can stop Him. The Lord can turn the light on anytime in our mind and make us see clearly what he is doing. God is in midst of our lives turning demons away from destroying our lives. He gave my one simple picture in my mind to see and the word floodgates. He was reminding me His grace and mercy on humanity and my life at the moment. I was not sure what He was referring to until one day it hit me that He was speaking of the fact that He alone had been and continue hold back demons from taking my life and yours. It was clear to me that God said, I hold the demons back from touching your life. In my mind, I was saying, they flee at His very command or thought. I learned that later He did more than hold them back. He destroyed them. He gave me the strength to realize that I am not defeated, the enemy has been defeated. He made me see that He alone stomped all of those demons at the root of sin and manipulation. God has my back on all things. I am more than a conqueror in Christ Jesus.

When you feel like the floodgates are being released to target your life and your family, remember that Jesus in on your side. Start praying in the spirit and use the word, for the word is your protection . The word of God is your sword and deliverance by the Holy Spirit. The word is our peace of mind when we are worried about things. Call on the name of Jesus to stop the flood waters and all the demons that come after you. Remember Jesus is the only one who holds all the flood gates of circumstances and enemy attacks. When it seems like life has unleased it's fury on you, call on the name of the Lord, Jesus save me from the floods of life. Jesus pick me up before I drawn in my own mess and circumstance that surround me. He is your strong tower in the middle of any raging storm. If it had not been for the blood of Jesus, we would be over run and destroyed by demons and the wrath of God. We owe the Lord our worship and praise from our hearts with all our might.

In Gen 9:11-13 Thus I establish my covenant with you: Never again shall the waters of the flood cut off all flesh; never again shall there be a flood to destroy the earth. And God said: This is the sign of the covenant which I make between Me and you, and every living creature that is with you, for perpetual generations:
I set my rainbow in the cloud, and it shall be for the sign of the covenant between Me and the earth.

MY COVENANT BLESSING

God is the controller in the seat for all things. The Psalmist tells us that He controls all the rain and waters of the earth. He even positions the sun and the moon according to His own power and purpose. Nothing can be established without Him. One of God's leading men was blessed beyond the floods of life and given the authority to replenish the earth by God Himself. God blessed Noah in the beginning because of His relationship and obedience to God. Because of Noah's obedience, God had a plan for Noah to build an Ark and save the lives of eight persons from the flood. We can easily see that God is in charge of all of the water on earth. We see it because He simply says there will never be another flood to destroy the earth. Historically we have seen floods come and go throughout many countries, the United States, Asia, and Europe. We have seen the devastation of them. Our merciful and graceful Lord has seen us through it all with His love and compassion. He has washed away our hurts and pains in those tough times of life. God promised not to flood the entire earth again and this earth has not been flooded entirely again. We need to remember why He flooded it in Noah's life time. The flood was ordered by God because of the wickedness and every evil imagination in man's heart at that time. Now why is He not flooding it again? Because He made a covenant with Noah and every living creature. His covenant has something to do with life preservation and life obedience and sacrifice. God already knew that He would not have to flood the ear\th again because He would send His son for our redemption. His plan of redemption was already in motion even before the flood. He would send His son to shed blood to wash our sin away with every evil imagination. Instead of washing us away in water, wiping out our lives God sent His son to wash us in the blood of the Lamb. Our God is merciful and compassionate in every way imaginable and incomprehensible. That is why we can glorify His name in the highest praise, alleluia.

HEBREWS 9:15-18 And for this reason He is the Mediator of the new covenant, by means of death for the redemptions of the transgressions under the first covenant, that those who are called may receive the promise of the eternal inheritance. For where there is a testament, there must also of necessity be the death of a testator. For a testament is in force after men are dead, since it has no power at all while the testator lives. Therefore not even the first covenant was dedicated without blood.

HEBREWS 9: 27-28 And as it is appointed for men to die once, but after this the judgment, so Christ was offered once, to bear the sins of many. To those who eagerly wait for Him He will appear a second time, apart from sin, for salvation.

HEBREWS 10: 14-19 for by one offering He has perfected forever those who are being sanctified. But the Holy Spirit also witnesses to us; for after he had said before, this is the covenant that I will make with them after those days, says the Lord: I will put My lawas into their hearts, and in their minds I will write them, then he adds Teir sins and their lawless deeds I will remember no more. Now where there is remission of these, there is no longer an offering for sin. Therefore, brethren, having boldness to enter the Holiest by the blood of Jesus, by a new and living way which He consecrated for us, through the veil, that is His flesh, and having a High Priest over the house of God.

Lord, you made the High Priest with Power to bless the house entirely.

CHAPTER 18

COVENANT KEEPERS

Genesis 15:18

Gen 17:10-11 God spoke to Abraham and said, This is My covenant which you shall keep between Me and you and your descendants after you: Every male child among you shall be circumcised; and you shall be circumcised in the flesh of your foreskins, and it shall be a sign of the covenant between me and you.

REVERSE: WALK IN CONVENANT WITH GOD, NOT WITH PEOPLE THAT HAVE MEAN YOU NO GOOD. YOU MEAN MORE THAN YOU KNOW TO GOD. WALK IN AGREEMENT. ACCEPT THE CONTRACT TO WALK IN BLESSINGS.

The Abrahamic covenant means: the covenant God made with Abraham in blessings. You should also recall the obedience that Abraham demonstrated before God. God saw it in his heart. God knew that Abraham would obey Him in faith.

God used covenants to identify relationships with Him and a chosen man of God. A covenant is an agreement between two parties. You must agree on a particular venture or form of business. God's ministry is business and has always been business. Are you in covenant with God? You are not the one who established the covenant. You just need to be in agreement with God. God did not ask Abraham to circumcise every male child. He said every male child among you shall be circumcised and you shall be circumcised in the flesh of your foreskin as well. It is significant that we be obedient to God. To remove the portion of your circumcised flesh meant that you would be clean in God's sight. You obeyed God with the most sensitive part of your body, the heart. God recognizes His people who are called by His name by relationship and identity.

See Genesis 12, 15:1-10, 20, 17, 18

Gen 22:15-17 Then the Angel of the Lord called to Abraham a second time out of heaven, and said: By myself I have sworn, says the Lord, because you have done this thing, and have not withheld your son, your only son vs17 "blessing I will bless you, and multiplying I will multiply your descendants as the stars of the heaven and as the sand which is on the seashore; and your descendants shall possess the gate of their enemies.

God approves of Abraham's actions. Here is a man who was willing to sacrifice his only son of his belief in God.

Galatians3:6-9 Just as Abraham believed God, and it was accounted to him for righteousness. Therefore know that only those who are of faith are sons of Abraham. And the Scripture foreseeing that God would justify the Gentiles by faith, preached the gospel to Abraham beforehand, saying, In you all the nations shall be blessed So then those who are of faith are blessed with believing Abraham

Hebrews 6:13-15 For when God made a promise to Abraham, because He could swear by no one greater, He swore by himself, saying Surely blessing I will bless you, and multiplying I will multiply you. And so, after he had patiently endured, he obtained the promise.

CHAPTER 19

GOD IS OUR TRUE DELIVERER

Exodus 24

Exodus 24:3 when Moses went and told the people all the Lord's words and laws, they responded with one every the Lord has said is voice. Everything he has said we will do.

God approves of Abraham's actions because he gave Moses the marching orders to tell Pharaoh. Here is a man who was willing to sacrifice his only son of his belief in God.

REVERSE OR TURN AROUND PAST SITUATION IN TO SOMETHING GOOD. REVERSE THE PHAROAH SPIRIT; THE ENEMY WAS YOUR DELIVER. TODAY MAKE GOD YOUR DELIVER. HE CAN DELIVER YOU OUT OF ALL BONDAGES AND SLAVE MENTALITY. GOD CAN DELIVER YOU FROM ANYTHING! HAVE FAITH AND BELIEVE. OBEDIENCE IS BETTER THAT SACRIFICE!

One of things about Moses time is that God honored Moses because of his obedience and his meekness and humility to follow the voice of God. Talk more about Moses shortly. I need to speak about Pharaoh since he is a character that most people really view as a extreme villain. All the time Pharaoh had God's people locked up in stiff and extreme bondage, his heart was satisfied and he was destined in his own mind not to change. In fact I recall viewing the old movie the Ten Commandments starring Charlton Heston and Ull Brynon, a classic. I probably remember as well. What made this such a classic is the series of events and it seem so real. It was also probably a classic in so many people's mind because it reflects freedom and more importantly a God who really shows a display of love and compassion, enough to set people free.

Moses even said to Pharaoh several times. "Let my people go." Throughout the entire course of events the plagues and death of first-born and the Red Sea being opened, Pharaoh heart was still hardened. You know it really does take God to change.

Hebrews 8:6 But now he has obtained a more excellent ministry , inasmuch as he is also Mediator of a better covenant, which was established on better promises. For if the first covenant would have been faultless, then no place would have been sought for the second.

CHAPTER 20

THE POWER OF SEED IN YOU

Gen 22:18 "In your seed all the nations of the earth shall be blessed, because you have obeyed my voice."

SEED BLESSING

God chose seed in the beginning. He wants people to observe his power. God gives the seed to bless. God blesses us as Abraham's seed because of his obedience. This is absolutely amazing. How can God bless everyone under one man of faith and obedience? But it shows us the power of God and how He views things in our lives. He reminds us that He can see every move that we make. He reminds us that He delights in us when we obey Him. If Abram had did the opposite of God, the outcome would have been different. We know it because the outcome with Adam was different. He made Abram the father of many nations because of his obedience. One thing for sure is that it makes me want to be more obedient to God. The more obedient I am, it seems the more blessings I get. Abram's name was change and He was blessed more than the stars in the sky. He was blessed more the sand on seashores. God is a God who promises and will never break His promises. God spoke and made a promise. He is not like man, He speaks His word and has to back it up. God is telling us that if you obey my voice, I will bless you. So then it is time to start being alert and listening to the voice of the Lord. Think about the things He just might ask of us.

Another blessing is when Jesus speaks while teaching the seed concept to His disciples in Mark 4:3-9 Listen Behold a sower went out to sow. And it happened as he sowed, that some seed fell by the wayside; and the birds of the air came and devoured it. Some fell on stony ground, where it did not have much earth; and immediately it sprang up because it had no debt of the earth. But when the sun was up it was scorched, and because it had no root it withered away. And some seed fell among thorns; and the thorns grew up and choked it, and it yielded no crop. But other seed fell on good ground and yield a crop that sprang up, increased and produced; some thirtyfold, some sixty, and some a hundred."

Mark 4:14 The sower sows the word. And these
are the ones by   the wayside where the word is sown.
When they hear, Satan comes immediately
and takes away the   word that was sown in their hearts.

Mark 4: 30-32 Then He said, to what shall we liken the kingdom of
God? Or with what parable shall we picture it?   "It is like a
mustard seed which, when it is sown on the ground, is smaller
than all the seeds on earth; but when it is sown, it grows up and
becomes greater than all herbs, and shoots out large branches,
so that the bids of the air may nest under its shade."

CHAPTER 21

BLOOD BROTHERS

Genesis 4:1-8

REVERSE: GOD WANTS YOU TO HAVE BLESSINGS FOR YOUR BLOOD BROTHER. DO NOT WALK IN JEALOUSY. BE A BLESSING TO GOD, BROTHER AND YOUR FAMILY BLOOD BROTHERS.

Blood brothers are bound to each other. Nothing is stronger than blood brothers but God. Your marriage is powerful, your friendships are powerful, and however blood brothers have a unique setting or footage when it comes to powerful connection.

Man puts forth maximum effort when he fights. God wants blood brothers and Christian brothers to maximize their efforts in fighting back the enemy by serving God. After all Jesus expressed the power of the Blood that washed away the sin of the world. It is a holy expression that is prayed about and helped by the Holy Spirit. But there is no one alive besides Jesus himself and the father who could express the power of the blood of the Jesus in its entirety. The blood is spoken of throughout eternity because it is the blood of God's only begotten Son. The blood has washed us whiter than snow. The blood has redeeming power; it has washed our sin away forever.

`

The blood is the most sacred and holy topic to speak of in all biblical doctrine. The blood is what saved the world and all that is in it. The blood is what gives us a purchased relationship with our Lord, Jesus. The blood is what makes Him the Lord of our lives. Without the blood there could be no remission of sin. God wants men in the church to be blood brothers.

CAIN AND ABEL THE SPLIT OF BLOOD BROTHERS

God allowed Adam and Eve to have their two sons. God simply blessed them. Cain and Abel presented God with sacrifices. Abel had a better sacrifice that pleased God. Cain was jealous. We should strive to present God our best sacrifice as we hear his voice telling us what to present. I believe you could offer the Lord your best sacrifice and be the most personal but if is not the right one, it is in vain. Abraham offered his best sacrifice, which was his son who he had waited for years. Yet he was willing to give him to God as an offering. God recognized Abrahams love for Him and God provided a ram in the bush and spared Isaac. That was a blessing to Abraham, the father of faith.

CHAPTER 22

THE BLOOD OF JESUS APPLIED

John 19: 34, Rev 7:9-17

Isaiah 53:5 But He was wounded for our transgressions, He was bruised for our iniquities; the chastisement for our peace was upon Him, And by His stripes we are healed.

The blood of the Lamb was slain for the remission of our sin came from the broken body of Jesus on Calvary. We first recognized His blood as He was beaten for the sin of the world. The enemy used whips to take flesh from His bruised body. The scriptures says by His stripes we are healed. It is referencing the blood that came from those flesh strips. Our Lord carried His cross with blood streaming from His body from head to His feet. We often sing a song call O the blood of Jesus, O the blood of Jesus, O the blood of Jesus, it will never lose its power. The blood of Jesus has all power. Nothing is more powerful than the blood of Jesus.

We are reminded in Corinthians 11:21-34 that Jesus' blood is the New Testament. Never again could priestly blood sacrifices be used to symbolize atonement for man's sin. No other blood can save us but the blood of Jesus, which has already cleansed us. Those that believe in Him through faith recognize that they are cleansed by His blood.

Exodus 20: 13 the doorpost is a foreshadow of things to come. When you see the blood, the death Angel will pass by.

Proverbs 11:11 by the blessing of the upright the city is exalted: but the mouth of the wicked overthrows it.

John 19: 17-18 And He, bearing His cross, went out to a place called the Place of Skull , which is called in Hebrew, Golgotha, where they crucified Him, and two others with Him, one on either side, and Jesus in the center .

John 19: 34 But one of the soldiers pierced His side with a spear, and immediately blood and water came out.

CHAPTER 23

SEALED BLESSINGS

EPHESIANS 1:13-14

REVERSE: GOD WANTS YOU TO BE SEALED BY HIS SPIRIT SO THAT NOTHING CAN TAKE YOU AWAY. YOU ARE SEALED BY THE POWER OF GOD.

SEALED BY THE HOLY SPIRIT OF PROMISE

Ephesians 1-13-14: In Him you also trusted, after you heard the word of truth, the gospel of your salvation; in whom also, having believed, you were sealed with the Holy Spirit of promise. Who is the guarantee of our inheritance until the redemption of the purchased possession, to the praise of His glory?

All believers should thank God for the seal of the Holy Spirit. If you can imagine a seal of pear jars, coke bottle seals and seals on food products to lock all the purities and freshness inside gives you somewhat of the importance of the Holy Spirit sealing you and I. We get used by God. We are sealed for God's purpose and he enemy has no power to break God's seal. Your seal is much like the seal of the Holy Spirit which means that God has already entered into your heart and now He lives on the inside. I was listening to a man tonight about a condition he had experienced. He spoke of the aneurysm in his head. The doctors told him that not only did he have one aneurysm to remove. It appears that we have two more operations to perform on you. The man immediately said that his life flashed before him. He said all of the good times and all of the bad times ran through his mind. Thanks to the Lord that we are not sealed with the bad time. But rather the bad times are forgiven and destroyed and not remembered by the Lord. We do not have to be confined to circumstances in our lives because circumstance will try to seal you with worldly ideas and past histories that bring you down. We need His Holy Word that speaks of His Divine Glory. We are covered in the blood of Jesus. Being covered in His blood gives us the assurance that we will be with Him forever because we are sealed with him. God is coming back for a church without spot or wrinkled. He will break the sky and those that know Him will be caught up in the air.

The Apostle Paul also mentioned a vital blessing in this scripture. He says having believed, you were sealed with the Holy Spirit of promise. The Holy Spirit came to help us receive every promise that God has given us. He will help us because God promise is a guaranteed of the inheritance from God Himself. Everything that God has for us will be for us no matter what the situation is in our lives. No one can take away His promises. When you are sealed with the Holy Spirit of Promise nothing can break the seal. Welcome to the family that is sealed by the power of the Holy Spirit. So rejoice and be exceedingly glad for the Lord has blessed you and He is on your side.

Revelations 7: 1-3 After these things I saw four angels standing at the four corners of the earth, holding the four winds of the earth, that the wind should not blow on the earth, on the sea, or on any tree. Then I saw another angel ascending from the east, having the seal of the living God. And he cried with a loud voice to the four angels to whom it was granted to harm the earth and the sea, saying, "Do not harm, the earth, the sea, or the trees till we have sealed the servants of our God on their foreheads."

God has sealed His servants to recognize who they are in His Kingdom. The seal is like no other seal. God sees His blood washed saints, those who chose God, accepted the Lord Jesus in their hearts. These are the people who truly serve God almighty. They are servants of God. Nowhere in history can anyone seal you to recognize you from harm and danger like God can. Everyone should thank God that His angels await His very command that they will not harm any of God's servants. God even made the angel wait till His saints are sealed on their foreheads. This is powerful because He ensures that His people that are called by His name are sealed. As Christians we should be trying to tell someone of the life changing savior and the future of living with Him forever. We should always encourage one another get a relationship that will secure your seal on the forehead with Christ Jesus. It is clearly understood that those who are sealed will reign with Him forever. What a sight to see in Heaven. He still loves His creation and identifies those that love Him. This seal that God put on believers that He himself has already predestined will reign with Him forever. The enemy can not take your seal away. Once God gives it, it is given forever as one of His very own family members.

Revelation 7:4-8 And I heard the number of them who were sealed. One hundred and forty - forty thousand of all the tribes of the children of Israel were sealed: of the tribe of Judah twelve thousand were sealed; of the tribe of Reuben twelve thousand were sealed; of the tribe of Gad twelve thousand were sealed; of the tribe of Asher twelve thousand were sealed; of the tribe of Naphtali twelve thousand were sealed; of the tribe of Manasseh twelve thousand were sealed; of the tribe of Simeon twelve thousand were sealed; of the tribe of Levi twelve thousand were sealed; of the tribe of Issachar twelve thousand were sealed; of the tribe of Zebulun twelve thousand were sealed; of the tribe of Joseph twelve thousand were sealed; of the tribe of Benjamin twelve thousand were sealed.

This is evidence that God started sealing people thousands of years ago. The God that we know as the bible clearly says, He never changes. He never sleeps nor slumbers as well. He is the God who is always watching us. Thanks be to the Lord our God who is holy and righteous. Of every tribe God blessed His servants with a seal. God loves to identify who is His. We need to understand that God said that He would bless Jacob and His seed. The scripture clearly shows the evidence of His promises. Our prayers go out to all generations forever.

Revelations 7: 13-17 Then one of the elders answered, saying to me, Who are these arrayed in white robes, and where did they come from? And I said to him, Sir, you know. So he said to me, These are the ones who come out of the great tribulation, and washed their robes and made them white in the blood of the Lamb. Therefore they are before the throne of God, and serve Him day and night in His temple. And He who sits on the throne will dwell among them. They shall neither hunger anymore nor thirst anymore; the sun shall not strike them, nor any heat; for the Lamb who is in the midst of the throne will shepherd them and lead them to living fountains of waters. And God will wipe away every tear from their eyes."

I need God my Lord to lead me and to console me in the midst of my troubles. I need Jesus and to experience His presence. I never knew anyone who could wipe away my tears. Sometimes I find myself driving down the express or even the back road and cry with tears of joy and wonder for a moment who will console me. Every time I need him.

Ephesians 1:3-10 Blessed be the God and Father of our Lord Jesus Christ, who has blessed us with every spiritual blessings in the heavenly places in Christ, Just as He chose us in Him before the foundation of the world, that we should be holy and without blame before Him in love, having predestined us to adoption as sons by Jesus Christ to Himself, according to the good pleasure of His will, to the praise of the glory of His grace, by which He made us accepted in the Beloved. In Him we have redemption through His blood, the forgiveness of sins, according to this riches of His grace which He made to abound toward us in all wisdom and prudence, having made known to us the mystery of His will, according to His good pleasure which He purposed in Himself, that in the dispensation of the fullness of the times He might gather together in one all things in Christ, both which are in heaven and which are on earth –in Him.

God allows us to know that we have Christians have all kinds of spiritual blessings. These spiritual blessings come directly from God because of favor in the Christian life.These spiritual blessings are beyond temporal blessings on earth such as material blessings. The Lord reveals to us that these spiritual blessings are the product of the Holy Spirit. Only the Holy Spirit can produce these spiritual blessings. The author tells us that these blessing are also activities that the believer has been lifted in Jesus Christ. In verse 4 he uses the word chose which in (Greek is eklegoman) means to pick out, to choose. The writer tells us that this deals with elective grace when it comes to believers. If had not been for Jesus there would be no grace, no selection before he foundation of the world. Because we are in Christ, nothing is too good nor too hard for God to grant to His Saints.

CHAPTER 24

BLOOD COVENANT BRINGS BLESSINGS

Hebrews 10:19-23 Therefore, brethren, having boldness to enter the Holiest by the blood of Jesus, by a new and living way which He consecrated for us, through the veil, that is, His flesh, and having a High Priest over the house of God, let us draw near with a true heart in full assurance of faith, having our hearts sprinkled from an evil conscience and our bodies washed with pure water. Let us hold fast the confession of our hope without wavering, for He who promised is faithful.

REVERSE: GOD WANTS US TO HAVE BOLDNESS BECAUSE YOU ARE COVERED IN THE BLOOD OF THE LAMB. WE ARE COVENANT PEOPLE OF GOD.

Let us be clear to the fact that we do not have the comprehensible knowledge to count and begin to know the richness and divine blessings of the blood that washed us whiter than snow. He is the God who makes covenant because He is the God of promise. God is the only one who can commit and keep His commitments absolutely spotless to the standard of His covenant and covenant love and power. A covenant is an agreement much like a contract. This is God solely in action taking His people back home to Him. Nothing is more powerful than the blood of Jesus Christ.

When you sign on the dotted line you gave your permission to agree to pay the entire loan back and to pay with interest. When you buy a house or a car, you made that purchase and it belongs to you alone. It means something to you because you bought the car or the home. It is yours and no one can take it away. Jesus is saying something here in the passage that you were bought with a price by His blood. In fact, the blood of Christ covers you completely. He bought you with His death, burial and resurrection. He used His own blood to do it. Nothing else could do it.

Hebrews 8:10 For this is the new covenant, that I will make with the house of Israel after those days, says the Lord: I will put My laws in their mind and write them on their hearts; and I will be their God, and they shall be My people.

This covenant is the new covenant and the most powerful covenant. It is the blood of the Lamb who takes away the sin of the world. The old way to covenant was from sacrifices of animals, bulls and goats and so forth for the purpose of our atonement. But please be not confused or ignorant. Jesus was the substitute for us. If He had not died, we would already be dead but the blood of Jesus, O' the blood of Jesus, O' the blood of Jesus will never lose it Power. O' the blood of Jesus, O' the blood of Jesus, O' the blood of Jesus will never lose it power. This song is undoubtedly one of the most popular songs ever sung. It seems that whenever God has need of this sung to be sang, He somehow pours out His anointing on a group of believers or somebody to sing it. The blood of Jesus is what cleansed us and washed us white as snow. Psalmist says wash me with hyssop so that I can be clean. The Psalmist also wrote that His blood is like crimson stain. We are always reminded that the blood of Jesus has power in it and gives us like. He washed our sin away in His blood. He redeemed us in His blood. When Jesus was crucified on the cross at Calvary, it was the blood that ran down His body to the ground and that blood has saved us from the wrath of God. The blood of Jesus showed us the power of His love for all humanity and every single people individually.

The blood of Christ Jesus reminds us of His great sacrifice and that we must anticipate in expectance of His great return to receive us.

The most exciting and stunning blessings are in His covenant blood blessings. Here the Apostle Paul speaks more about His covenant. In God's covenant, not only does he want us to be in His covenant, He wants us to commune with Him in His covenant. There is no other power than His

blood. Saints throughout the entire world is a part of communing with God because believe and profess and fall under the authority of His covenant. The Apostle Paul writes in Hebrews about God's covenant.

Hebrews 9:15 And for this reason he is the Mediator of the new covenant, by mans of death, for the redemption of the transgressions under the first covenant, that those who are called may receive the promise of the eternal inheritance.

CHAPTER 25

GLORIFY GOD

John 16

REVERSE: Start living your life where you glorify God in the things you do. Glorifying God demonstrates to Him your character, who you stand for and who you express sincere love for. God is the answer.

The first thing we must understand is that in John God reveals that the Holy Spirit is God's agent to help us glorify Him. The point in this passage is that you glorify God and nothing else in your life. Do not glorify your children, wife nor the husband because you make them gods before God. Therefore he is not pleased.

We do not have the power within our individual ability to do it. We must be empowered and led by the Holy Spirit on the inside of us to glorify God. So we you know that you are giving God the glory for the many anchored blessings and the now blessings in your life, please know that the Holy Spirit is present and operating at every moment. It's okay to cry right now if your heart tells you to because of His goodness. I know how you feel when you feel so rich and deeply blessed in His presence.

John 16: 8-14 And when He has come, he will convict the world of sin, and of righteousness, and of judgment: of sin, because they do not believe in Me; of righteousness, because I go to My Father and you see Me no more; of judgment, because the ruler of this world is judged. However, when He, the Spirit of truth, has come, He will guide you into all truth; for He will not speak on His own authority, but whatever He hears He will speak; and He will tell you things to come. He will glorify Me, for He will take of what is Mine and declare it to you. All things that the Father has are mine. Therefore I said that He will take of Mine and declare it to you.

To shout at the man running down the field with a pig skin is exciting and fun to thousands around the world. Look at your television set and see the excitement and celebration when someone scores. When the touchdown is made, who gets the glory? Is the scorer, the team, the coach or is it God. When the super bowl ring and the trophy is delivered to the winning team in the season, who gets the glory? Is it the scorers, the team, or the coach? And the same applies to the home run hitters and all of the sports that exist. With our winning team having done what it takes, we are happy at heart. There is a time to glorify God and that time is for you to know individually. For the believer, we believe in glorifying Him at all times. In fact, we glorify Him because we know that the Spirit leads us to doing so. We glorify Him because He is the one who blessed us. He is also the one and only true God who delivered us from our death. It is easy to glorify things such as a house, car, money, relationships and gold and silver. So God sent us the Holy Spirit of truth so that we can evade those temptations and our flesh can rebuke in the name of Jesus. We glorify Jesus because He first loved us and washed us clean. He washed us whiter than snow.

CHAPTER 26

A GOOD WITNESS REVERSES LIVES

Acts 1

Act 1:8 but you shall receive power when the Holy Spirit has come upon you; and you shall be witnesses to Me in Jerusalem, and in all Judea and Samaria, and to the end of the earth.

REVERSE: GOD WANTS YOU TO RECEIVE POWER. HE WANTS YOU TO HAVE GOD'S POWER THAT ENABLES AND EQUIPS YOU TO WITNESS THE LOVE OF JESUS CHRIST. ACT OUT BOLDLY.

Before you get to church on Sunday, remember what your mission was all week long. It was to get 2- 100 people into the church to hear the word of God. Islam, Mormons, and Jehovah Witnesses all make extreme efforts to get people in that religion. One of thing that you may not be aware of is that people are falling away from the Christian church and falling for cults, like witchcraft and all kinds of cults involving false prophets and false apostles and false beliefs with bad doctrine that has no truth in it, nor is it the word of God. Get out of that ministry. You are not bound to it. Leave today and find a true church with sound doctrine. Those are false organization with ministries in disguise. Be careful because there are many activities or church like appearance organization going on but they really have nothing to do with Jesus Christ church. It is time for you to witness and get at least 1, 20, 40, 100, 1000 or more to get them into church where the word of God is being preached. Tell them Romans 10:9. Tell them to meet with the Pastor with a third party to know what you are getting into or visit and observe. Do not allow itchy ears or your emotions overtake you and join out of feeling good. Seek the Holy Spirit. It is critical at this point because of the end times approaching that you get into the word of God and become servants for God. Being a doer of the faith is power as in becoming a witness as good equips you is one of the highest privileges in ministry.

It is absolutely amazing how people can enter a temple with a mind to worship and praise. I believe it is a blessing to have such ability under the power of the Holy Ghost. If we have that attitude to enter in with thanksgiving and praise to Almighty God, He certainly wants us to recognize those people in need. Anointed men and women should be the first to stop on the street and bring in those that are lost.

The point is that God made us witnesses under the power of the Holy Spirit. So we must exhibit that power on the outside of the church and it will be on the inside. We live in a constant struggle and battle much like the lame man. His struggle that kept him from witnessing was his cripple and maimed body. Yet, he had faith to believe that God could heal through men sent on his path. When this lame man was healed by the touch of God through Peter's hand he witnessed with the utmost joy. He was healed by his faith but more importantly by the name of Jesus Christ because Peter said, silver and gold, I do not have but what I have I give you, in the name of Jesus Christ of Nazareth, rise up and walk. Peter and John walked in their witness. Acts 3:1 Now Peter and John went up together to the temple at the hour of prayer, the ninth hour. And a certain man lame from his mother's womb was carried whom they laid daily at the gate of the temple which is called beautiful, to ask alms from those who entered the temple;

This was an amazing miracle done by these men. God wants this kind of witnessing. One of the biggest obstacles and disruptive obstacles when it comes to helping someone get close Jesus Christ is a jealous spirit. When the lame man was healed, Peter did not get jealous of John, John did not get jealous of Peter. They were on one accord and out to witness in the power of the Holy Spirit. Too often churches have issue with so called members or so called Christians or even non-believers with a jealous spirit. This spirit is simply of the devil. People leave church because they have a jealous spirit and other reasons, however, most of the time they cannot even recognize that they are jealous. What does jealous mean? You despise what someone else has that is good and you want it. It also means you hate the fact that some people have an ability or possession better than yours in your mind. Example, there may be 100 people in the choir but three lead singers have magnificent voices. When Pam Wright sings, the other two, Janice Frazier and Michelle Stewart get mad because they have been there longer and can't stand someone else to get applause. They want all the attention so they start whispering and talking, and giggling about the Pam as she sings so superb, bringing the house down. This is the kind of behaviors that breaks up choirs and interrupts worshipping God. The problem with the other two singers is that Pam Wright is new to the church and just joined three weeks ago and going full steam in service. How does it impact the church? In some churches it causes divide, the people that became jealous does not realize that that spirit of jealousy inside them was not of God. In fact it was against God's witness and blessings. What are the signs of jealousy? Stop coming to church because another woman or man sings just as good as you sing. Another one is that you feel threatened by someone else's ability and when no one else is even thinking about you limiting yourself. Another one is you makes excuses and blames others for your weakness and allowing confusion to take over you. Simply put, you are the culprit. You allowed that demonic spirit of jealousy to enter your mind and heart. Can you reverse this jealous spirit in a good righteous spirit? Yes with the help of the Holy Spirit. Jesus specializes in reverse demonic spirits. He cast them out in Mark 5. Simply ask God to remove the spirit from you and believe have faith that God has removed. Start walking with a new spirit man, a new spirit woman.

CHAPTER 27

GOD'S POWER REIGNING IN YOU!

Acts 2

Acts 2:1-4 When the Day of Pentecost had fully come they were all with one accord in one place. And suddenly there came a sound from heaven, as of a rushing mighty wind, and it filled the whole house where they were sitting. Then there appeared to them divided tongues, as of fire, and one sat upon each of them. And they were all filled with the Holy Spirit and began to speak with other tongues, as the Spirit gave them utterance.

REVERSE: GOD WANTS YOU TO HAVE A HOLY SPIRIT EXPERIENCE TODAY SO YOU CAN REIGN WITH JESUS CHRIST.

Reigning means there is a period in which a person or thing is dominant, ruler, authority influential and powerful. Reigning with God is being in the presence and power as we influence others through Jesus Christ. He reigns and nothing can stop his power and influencing power. We live and reign with Jesus Christ.

You have been identified as one of God's people that will reign with Him. God was using the day of Pentecost to show forth his power in his church and saints. Get this piece because people need to know that Pentecost was on that day. God was revealing power pouring out on his people, equipping them for the work of the ministry and church. The Holy Spirit wants us to know that a Pentecost like experience is available every day. The Holy Spirit is present today to change live, cause people to speak in tongues and empowering saints. People need to know that God is still pouring out His spirit. He simply makes Himself available for acceptance to the heart. This is exciting what the writer is saying. Pentecost means 50 days and its broken down into three distinct identities and functions. It represents the day of the feast. God wants His people to be on one accord. This one accord expresses unity in Jesus Christ. Certainly the enemy the devil will try to conquer and divide the church and separate you from the ministry. Church members need to be on one accord to express power and agreement in prayer and ministry. There will be many on one accord with Him. The Holy Spirit reveals himself in a blessed way.

Acts 2:16-21 But this is what was spoken by the prophet Joel: And it shall come to pass in the last days, says God, That I will pour out of My Spirit on all flesh; Your sons and your daughters shall prophesy, Your young men shall see visions, Your old men shall dream dreams, And on My menservants and on My maidservants I will pour out My Spirit in those days; And they shall prophesy. I will show wonders in heaven above and signs in the earth beneath: blood and fire and vapor of smoke.

God wants His people to know Him and trust Him. Our Lord is expressing such an blessing in our lives that we can comprehend the majesty and honor and power and might. I thank God that He will pour out His Spirit on all flesh because the day is coming.

Acts 2:41 Then those who gladly received his word were baptized; and that day about three thousand souls were added to them.

Acts 4:31: And when they had prayed, the place where they were assembled together was shaken; and they were filled with the Holy Spirit, and they spoke the word of God with boldness.

2 Corinthians12:1, It is doubtless not profitable for me to boast I will come to visions and revelations of the Lord.

2 Corinthians 12:4 how he was caught up into Paradise and heard inexpressible words, which it is not lawful for a man to utter.

2 Corinthians 12: 7. And lest I should be exalted above measure by the abundance of the revelation a thorn in the flesh was given to me, a messenger of Satan to buffet me, lest I be exalted above measure.

CHAPTER 28

FAITH REVERSES SITUATIONS

HEBREWS 11

Acts 10:44-48 While Peter yet spoke these words, the Holy Ghost fell on all them which heard the word. And they of the circumcision which believed were astonished, as many as came with Peter, because that on the Gentiles also was poured out the gift of the Holy Ghost. For they heard them speak with tongues, and magnify God. Then answered Peter, Can any man forbid water, that these should not be baptized, which have received the Holy Ghost as well as we? And he commanded them to be baptized in the name of the Lord. Then prayed they him to tarry certain days.

REVERSE: FAITH IN THE SPIRIT REVERSE SITUATIONS THAT ARE NOT OF GOD. REVERSE FROM YOU OLD NATURE THAT IS NOT OF GOD TO A SPIRIT FILLED, FAITH FILL MAN AND WOMEN OF GOD

FILLED IN THE SPIRIT

When we get filled in the Spirit, we go through things that impact in a tremendous way.
We need this infilling because we need to be under the influence of God in all facets of life. If you think God does not know about it you are wrong.

Ephesian 5:18 and do not be drunk with wine, in which is dissipation; but be filled with the Spirit.

I just spoke a young lady about her needs to survive and take care of family. She needs resources such water, milk, food, and wants to move in now because she did not understand the extent of self-reliance and responsibility. Faith is absent from her mind at this moment. Most people use the popular scripture in Phil 4:19, God will supply all of my needs according to his riches in glory. She had an apartment the other day for $675 a month the other day but she lost it. She did not have the deposit and did not have a job. She desperately wants to move in. My heart is saying allow it for a month but it is also saying pay for the new apartment that she researched. We need to bless her either way it goes. I prefer the plan you spoke of. So let me know what I need to do to resolve it. I am not hard hearted about any of it. I just need to make sure peace is maintained in the house at the same time she must be taken care of. The other grandmother is not answering her call. I want to close it out and still let her know that she is loved. I love my family. At the same time I have to maintain order and discipline in my house. Every man need a good wife to help him with these obligations. If you do not work as a team in your marriage, it is destined to struggle or even break up. God is your answer in all respects. Everything we are surrounded with comes back to whether you have faith in God.

GOD'S WARRIORS OF FAITH

Faith is the foundation of the bible as it relates to believers in the Father, the Son and Holy Spirit. Faith is not limited. Faith get results Faith centers on the will of God. Faith is the center along with the love of God. It believes without any doubt that God is God and there is no other God. God exist beyond comprehension. Christian faith operates in the supernatural and the natural because God made Spirit and flesh. We crucify the flesh to stay connected to God who is invisible yet is as real as you and I can see each other. Faith is the central believe of Christianity. It is the pulse and central nerve center of our spiritual walk with Christ Jesus. You must have faith to walk with Jesus. It is almost the same as Jesus telling Nicodemus that you must be born again. You can not enter the kingdom of heaven without this kind of faith. There is another story about fasting in Matthew 9. You cannot do miracles without this kind of faith unless you are fasting and praying. Faith works with fasting and prayer. We must understand that without faith it is according to Luke, "It is impossible to please God" Faith brings about manifestation because you believe that God can, He will demonstrate it. Most of us use faith with the passage in Philippian 4:13, I can do all things through Christ who strengthens me in Christ Jesus. It was faith that impacted all of Jesus disciples. It was faith that Jesus personally had Himself to carry His cross and be crucified and raised from the dead. Faith is the foundation for life.

MUSTARD SEED FAITH

MATTHEW 17:20-21 And Jesus said unto them, Because of your unbelief: for verily I say unto you, If ye have faith as a grain of mustard seed, ye shall say unto this mountain, Remove hence to yonder place; and it shall remove; and nothing shall be impossible unto you. Howbeit this kind goeth not out but by prayer and fasting.

One of the major problems in Christianity is that people get mixed up with how much faith they have. God is looking for genuine Holy Ghost believing faith. Again as in the previous chapter, God said, I dealt you a measure of faith.

The challenge is that anyone can be filled with faith. The question is what kind of faith is it? Is the faith that God see in your heart and life.

THROUGH TRIBULATIONS

ROMANS 5:1-5 Therefore being justified by faith, we have peace with God through our Lord Jesus Christ: By whom also we have access by faith into this grace wherein we stand, and rejoice in hope of the glory of God. And not only so, but we glory in tribulations also: knowing that tribulation worketh patience; And patience, experience; and experience, hope: And hope maketh not ashamed; because the love of God is shed abroad in our hearts by the Holy Ghost which is given unto us.

You are given access to the Lord. Your faith is measured or analyzed by the enemy every day. The enemy cause tribulations and things that you know are ungodly to stump you. Because I know that His power works on the inside and outside, I rely on Him. Listen, God wants to reverse your living and attitude when it comes to faith, peace, and success and the hope of glory. God is asking us to activate the faith he gave us. You can do it because of the power of the Holy Spirit in your life. We are justified meaning not guilty of sin. We know we are justified because of the faith we walk in of Jesus Christ. Tribulations have no power to shake you from your Christian belief. When I lost my parents, the enemy thought he almost had me until I called on the name of Jesus Christ. Just in case you really did not understand me calling on the name of Jesus Christ, let me simply explain, Jesus owns the entire world.

There are many faith stories. Hebrews 11 lists all of the heroes of faith. One that was unusual to me is about Zachius. You might remember Zachius. He was a tax collector. He was also the one who climb a tree to see Jesus coming toward his house. To his amazement, Jesus was headed directly to his house. He was not passing by. He came to Zachius house to for a meal. When Jesus stopped at Zachius house, it sparked all kinds of discussion and judgment. Jesus did not come by Zachius house to judge a tax collector who had done wrong. He came by to offer reconciliation, restoration, love and faith in the son of God.

The fact that Jesus stopped by to visit Zachius was enough to blow Zachius' mind. Jesus visit to his house was so powerful that Zachius realized that he was in the presence of holiness. To that point he offered to give back all with additional portion that he took in taxes. Jesus has that effect on people. His love will shine right through each of us in Spirit and truth because that is who He is. What about your house today? Will you ask Jesus to visit? Well, if you do not ask Him, He will come anyway because He is everywhere in Spirit.

CHAPTER 29

HOLY SPIRIT MOVING IN MY LIFE

There are many people who do not know who God is and the answer to the beginning or God and this world. John gives an answer that will undoubtedly answer questions pertaining to such. In this scripture you see our Lord God in His fullness. This will enlighten you to why you are blessed by the word of God.

John 1:1-5 says, in the beginning was the Word, and the Word was with God, and the Word was God. He was in the beginning with God. All things were made through Him, and without Him nothing was made that was made. In Him was life, and the life was the light of men. And the light shines in the darkness, and the darkness did not comprehend it.

God is according to John pre-existent. Before time could exist God was already in existence. Nothing made God. He is the creator and ruler of all that exist. Our Lord God made all things. God is sovereign and omnipotent. He is all powerful and everywhere. God spoke things into existence for His pleasure and only His purpose. He is God by Himself. He reigns and rules all.

John 1:17 For the law was given through Moses, but grace and truth came through Jesus Christ. No one has seen God at any time. The only begotten Son, who is in the bosom of the Father, He has declared Him.

Revelations 19:12 His eyes were like a flame of fire, and on His head were many crowns. He had a name written that no man knew except Himself. He was clothed with a robe dipped in blood, and His name is called the Word of God.

In Revelations, we see Jesus in the eyes of John. The picture of Jesus is as no man had ever seen Him in the flesh with that appearance.

Jerimiah 1:9-10. Then the Lord put forth His hand and touched my mouth, and the Lord said to me: Behold I have put my words in your mouth. See, I have this day set you over the nations and over the kingdoms, to root out and to pull down, to destroy and to throw down, to build and to plant.

God touched Jerimiah and put His words in him. Anyone can touch you but anyone cannot put their word in you. God placed His word in Jerimiah so he could do God's will. What was amazing to me is the fact that Jerimiah recognizes the fact that God touched him. Many people can miss that. We must be careful to acknowledge when God touches us. Specifically in this case we need to know that God has given us His word. So we must trust Him. Thy word O'Lord I hid in my heart that I might not sin against you.

POUR OUT MY SPIRIT

JOEL 2: 28-29 And it shall come to pass afterward that I will pour out My Spirit on all flesh; Your sons and your daughters shall prophesy, Your old men shall dream dreams, Your young men shall see visions. And also on my menservants and on my maidservants I will pour out My Spirit in those days.

God knows exactly who He will pour His spirit out on in the last days. In this passage, He mentions several people to pour out His Spirit. Look out because your son and daughter will prophesy. Be prepared because young men will begin to see visions and it is God really mission, worship, obedience in service for those He called. God is very adamant about pouring out His Spirit. The picture I get is that God is pouring out His unlimited power and faith on His people . He equips His people for revivals all over the city. We can not run like Jonah.

144

CHAPTER 30

THE WORD IS POWERFUL

John 15

THE BLESSING OF ABIDING IN HIM

John 15:7 says, If you abide in Me, and My words abide in you, you will ask what you desire, and it shall be done for you.

REVERSE: THE WORD REVERSES SITUATIONS BECAUSE IT GIVES FAITH AND GROWTH AND BLESSINGS.

In John 1:1-3 In the beginning was the word and the word was with God and the word was God. The word of God is speaking to us today to abide in Him. Abiding (Remaining) in Christ means that you believe that Jesus is the Son of God and that He is your Lord and Savior. So then we stay connected to Him because we claim Jesus to be in our hearts. We are positioned in Jesus by the power of the Holy Ghost and in His will because we willingly abide in our Lord Jesus.

In John 15:1-7 We see ourself as branches connected to our sourc, he vine and the Father who is the vinedresser. It is Jesus and His word that prunes us so we can serve and please Him faithfully under the anointing.

I Samuel 15:22 reminds us that we should be obedient . He says, "obedience is better than sacrifice." The Lord Himself stated you will ask what you desire, and it shall be done for you. If you take this scripture and trust God you will begin to see changes in your life and those around you. When Saul was king, God gave him instruction to take the land and destroy all things on it. However, he disobeyed God. God took away his anointing and his kingship because of his disobedience to God. God took away His kingship. King Saul got in trouble for the word says, And Saul said unto Samuel, I have sinned, because I feared the people and obeyed Their voice. You see King Saul was to remain under God's authority and under God's control. He took things into his own hand and made a terrible mistake. He disobeyed God and each time it was because He feared the people. We have to walk in the spirit of Christ Jesus to be obedient to His word. King Saul lost his position because he was disobedient.

Lately, I have been seeing more and more of the positioning myself in Christ. In Samuels story, I am seeing that obedience is the key principle in positioning myself. When you know who you are, you can position yourself by the aid of the Holy Spirit. John shows us a clear picture of the branch and the vine. Each vine is well connected and positioned for the glory of God. I believe that the seed of that tree had to be place properly and positioned so that it would grow and take root. Notice something. No one never went back to alter the seed that was placed in the ground to grow this tree. If someone had gone back after the years the tree could have been dead.

ABIDE IN HIM

JOHN 15:4 Abide in me, and I in you. As the branch cannot bear fruit of itself, except it abide in the vine; no more can ye, except ye abide in me.

Abiding means spending time with someone on an intimate level and remaining connected. When you abide in Him, you might as well get ready to have a breakthrough. Jesus said in John 14, in my house are many mansions; I go to prepare a place for you. If you abide in Him, certainly there is a mansion laid up in heaven.

King Solomon says in Proverbs 3:5 Trust in the Lord with all your heart and lean not to your own understanding and acknowledge him in all ways and He will direct your path. I believe that Jesus wants us to trust him completely without holding back anything. And treat His word the as the only authority. He wants you to know His word because life is in His words and the power to change people lives are in His word.

The word says in Act 2:8 … and you shall be witnesses to Me in Jerusalem, and in all Judea and Samaria, and to the end of the earth.

CHAPTER 31

BLESSED BY HEARING THE WORD

ROMANS 10

GOD WANTS ALL OF HIS CHILDREN TO HEAR HIM THROUGH THE WORD.

REVERSE: THE PENETRATING POWER OF THE WORD OF GOD GETS ON THE INSIDE OF PEOPLE TO DELIVER THEM FROM SIN AND BONDAGE, THEN BRINGS THEM INTO THE MARVELOUS LIGHT OF JESUS CHRIST AND SALVATION

THE WORD GRIPS AND ANCHORS

Romans 10:8-14: But what does it say? "The word is near you, in your mouth and in your heart" that is, the word of faith, which we preach): that if you confess with your mouth the Lord Jesus and believe in your heart that God has raised Him from the dead, you will be saved. For with the heart one believes unto righteousness, and with the mouth confession is made unto salvation. For the scripture says "Whoever believes on Him will not be put to shame." For there is no distinction between Jews and Greek, for the same Lord over all is rich to all who call upon Him. For whoever calls on the name of the Lord shall be saved."

Have you ever heard a debating team? Great debate teams use words to impact others as they listen. Words that debate teams use in their persuasive arguments usually grip at the hearts of components as well as the audience. Almost all people in society are impacted when they hear the word of God. It is to the benefit of everyone that they take in scriptures to receive blessings. If you are not careful you can be persuaded with the voices that has no Godly word in it. Be careful who you listen to-seek God for advice. So many people generally mean good but sometimes, there can be a slip up. We should always listen real good so we can receive what is really being spoken to us by the Lord.

Romans 10:14-15 How then shall they call on Him in whom they have not believed? And how shall they believe in Him of whom they have not heard? And how shall they hear without a preacher? And how shall they preach unless they are sent? As it is written: How beautiful are the feet of those who preach the gospel of peace, Who bring glad tidings of good things!

Hebrews 4: 12 For the word of God is living and powerful, and sharper than any two-edged sword, piercing even to the division of soul and spirit, and of joints and marrow, and is a discerner of the thoughts and intents of the heart.

No wonder you can't help but be anchored in the word of God. It is living and powerful than a two edged sword. Do you know what a two edged sword is?

John 15:7-8 if you abide in me, and my words abide in you, you will ask what you desire, and it shall be done for you. By this my Father is glorified, that you bear much fruit; so you will be my disciples.

When the word abides in you, you will never ever be the same again. Do not take my word for it, just experience the word for yourself and see what happens. It will not matter what other people say or do the word will change you.

Proverbs 30:5 says that every word of God is pure; He is a shield to those who put their trust in Him. Do not add to His word, lest He rebuke you, and you be found a liar.

2 Timothy 3:16-17 All scripture is given by inspiration of God, and profitable for doctrine, reproof, for correction, for instruction in righteousness, that the man of God might be complete, thoroughly equipped for every good work.

John 17:17: Sanctify them by your truth. Your word is truth. As You sent Me into the world, I also have sent them into the world. And for their sakes I sanctify myself, that they also may be sanctified by the truth. I do not pray for these alone, but also for those who will believe In Me through their word; that they all may be one, as You, Father, are in Me, and I in You; that they also may be one in Us, that the world may believe that You sent Me. Father, I desire that they also whom You gave Me may be with Me where I am, that they may behold My glory which You have given Me; for You loved Me before the foundation of the world. O'righteous Father! The world has not known You, but I have known You; and these have known that You sent Me.

ROMANS 1:16-23 For I am not ashamed of the gospel of Christ,[1] for it is the power of God to salvation for everyone who believes, for the Jew first and also for the Greek. For in it the righteousness of God is revealed from faith to faith; as it is written, "The just shall live by faith.

For the wrath of God is revealed from heaven against all ungodliness and unrighteousness of men, who suppress the truth in unrighteousness because what may be known of God is manifest in them, for God has shown it to them. For since the creation of the world His invisible attributes are clearly seen, being understood by the things that are made, even His eternal power and Godhead, so that they are without excuse, because, although they knew God, they did not glorify Him as God, nor were thankful, but became futile in their thoughts, and their foolish hearts were darkened. Professing to be wise, they became fools, and changed the glory of the incorruptible God into an image made like corruptible man—and birds and four-footed animals and creeping things.

·CHAPTER 32

SPEAK THE WORD

Hebrews 4

SPEAK TO MY HEART

In the book of *Hebrews 4:12, the Apostle Paul writes, For the word of God is living and powerful, and sharper than any two-edged sword, piercing even to the division of soul and spirit, and of joints and marrow, and is discerner of the thoughts and intents of the hearts.*

REVERSE THE TIDE: SPEAK TO MY HEART LORD JESUS. GET MY ATTENTION SO I CAN SERVE YOU.

I could not help but to think that God wants us to speak with passion to our spouses. Our Lord God spoke the world into existence and the entire world was formed in six days. He rested on the seventh day, Sabbath and sanctified it. The blessing is God's power unleashed on His people. God blesses us with the ability and power to speak things into existence and things such as sin out of our live. He gave His saints that kind of power under His authority.

THE POWER OF THE TONGUE

James 3:5-8 Even so the tongue is a little member, and boasteth great things. Behold, how great a matter a little fire kindleth! And the tongue is a fire, a world of iniquity: so is the tongue among our members, that it defileth the whole body, and setteth on fire the course of nature; and it is set on fire of hell. For every kind of beasts, and of birds, and of serpents, and of things in the sea, is tamed, and hath been tamed of mankind: But the tongue can no man tame; it is an unruly evil, full of deadly poison.

The tongue has the power of life and death. God never put the tongue in our mouths to destroy one another. We have it for a purpose. More importantly, we have it to glorify God in songs, and music and witnessing to others. God can control the tongue. Ask Him to guide the tongue because self will get off track because of pride and wrong understanding of the word of God.

I believe that we need to speak life into people circumstances. We speak life by the power of His word. We speak His word to people to heal people. That is what those who are saved do to reflect the Lord's spirit and word inside of them. So often people are judged and put down for so many reasons. But Thanks to God for His word that has the authority and power to divide soul and spirit. That tells me that when we speak this word of wisdom, this word of healing, this word of love, the word of joy , the word peace, a word of restoration, a word of reconciliation, a word of praise something happens. We might not see it when we want to see it. But God is on time with the results. He is healing someone right now because of the faith and power of a saint's prayer.

THE WORDS OF HEALING CAN BLESS

There is another powerful meaning of the word and that is the healing power of the word. Nothing else can take the place of it. Jesus spoke the word of healing in the life of ten men who had leprosy. In the Old Testament there was a man who had leprosy by the name of Naman who was given instruction by the man of God Elijah to go and dip in the Jordon seven times for his healing. Both times healing was spoken. Today when we get into our own pity parties and seemingly unhopeful recovery circumstances, we need to call out healing in the name of Jesus. Isaiah 53:5 tells us by His stripes we are healed. We need to speak daily. Psalms 103:3-4 says who forgives all your iniquities and Who heals all your diseases, Who redeems your life from destruction. God continues to bless us more and more each day and by the moment of our lives. James 5 tells that the effectual fervent prayer of a

152

righteous man aileth much. There is power in the word when even a righteous man speaks the word in prayer.

James 5: 14-15 is any sick among you? let him call for the elders of the church; and let them pray over him, anointing him with oil in the name of the Lord: And the prayer of faith shall save the sick, and the Lord shall raise him up; and if he have committed sins, they shall be forgiven him.

James 5: 16 Confess your faults one to another, and pray one for another, that ye may be healed. The effectual fervent prayer of a righteous man availeth much.

Psalm 119:11 Your word I have hidden in my heart, That I might not sin against you. Blessed are you O' Lord. Teach me your statutes.

It is so important to hide the word in our hearts. Not only does it help us from sinning against God, the word helps us through burdens. James says I count all joy when I fall into divers temptation know that trying of my faith

One thing that helps us is when we approach God. Hebrews 4:16 says Let us therefore come boldly to the throne of grace, that we may obtain mercy and find grace to help in time of need.

A powerful and meaningful approach would be to take God's word to the throne. Then from the heart speak to Him His word. He will answer because He is a God who cannot refuse His word and He cannot lie. The word speaks directly to your heart. When it does the presence of God moves on your behalf.

CHAPTER 33

WORSHIP ONLY GOD!

Revelations 11

GOD WANTS US TO TAP IN TO HEAVEN'S BLESSINGS

Revelations 11:16-17 And the twenty-four elders who sat before God on their thrones fell on their faces and worshiped God, saying; "We give you thanks, O Lord God Almighty, The One who is and who was and who is to come, Because You have taken Your great power and reigned.

REVERSE: YOUR LIFE IS SUPPOSED TO BE COMPOSED OF WORSHIPPING AND SERVING GOD. WORSHIP GOD AND WATCH BLESSINGS FLOW IN YOUR LIFE.

There is an inexpressible joy when you worship God. If you ever wanted to see yourself worshipping and glorifying God, try putting yourself in the scene of the scripture above. Take special note to what these Elders did. God requires that we worship Him with this kind of commitment and service. We must glorify Him. These men fell on their faces before God signifying the Lord's holiness and their absolute sincerity and humility in worshiping God. These men are blessed to be in heaven on their faces before God himself. Worship helped to get them in heaven. Worship is required in earth and in heaven. So anyone can see the significance of bowing down and worshipping the only one and true God who sits on the throne in heaven. I believe that the Lord desires all of His people to have a place in heaven where they can worship him. I believe that if we fall on our faces daily God Almighty will see us and it will be pleasing in His sight.

REVERSE THE TIDE

Ephesians 1:3 –10 blessed be the God and Father of our Lord Jesus Christ, who has blessed us with every spiritual blessings in the heavenly places in Christ.

Revelations 19:9 then he said to me, Write Blessed are those who are called to the marriage supper of the Lamb! " And he said to me, These are the true sayings of God."

Revelations 19:10 And I fell at his feet to worship him. But he said to me, See that you do not do that! I am your fellow servant, and of your brethren who have the testimony of Jesus. Worship God! For the testimony of Jesus is the spirit of prophecy."

Revelations 19:11 Now I saw heaven opened and behold, a white horse. And he who sat on him was called Faithful and True, and in righteousness He judges and makes war.

Revelations 19:12 His eyes were like a flame of fire, and on His head were many crown. He had a name written that no man knew except Himself. He was clothed with a robe dipped in blood, and His name is called the Word of God.

Revelation 21:1 now I saw a new heaven and a new earth, for the first heaven and the first earth had passed away. Also there was no more sea. Then I, John, saw the holy city, New Jerusalem, coming down out of heaven from God, prepared as a bride adorned for her husband.

CHAPTER 34

FILLED WITH OVERFLOWING JOY

Revelation 22

REVERSE: GOD WANTS HIS PEOPLE TO BE FILLED WITH JOY IN WORSHIP

Revelation 22: 8-9 Now I, John, saw and heard these things. And when I heard and saw, I fell down to worship before the feet of the angel who showed me these things. Then he said to me, " See that you do not do that. For I am your fellow servant, and of your brethren the prophets, and of those who keep the words of this book. Worship God."

John tells us that He worshipped God in the vision God gave him. The angel responded to John not to worship him, but worship God. It was not that John was worshipping the angel but He was in such awe that He fell down to worship God mighty acts. He was overwhelmed and filled with unspeakable joy. I believe that when people realize who God is and begin to worship Him they will experience a joy like John's joy in the presence of God.

Psalm 145:1 I will extol you, my God, O King; And I will bless Your name forever and ever. Every day I will bless you, and I will praise Your name forever and ever. Great is the Lord and greatly to be praised; and his greatness is unsearchable.

James 1:2 my brethren, count it all joy when you fall into various trials, knowing that the testing of your faith produces patience.

The Lord wants us to know that we will have trials. But worship God! Some trials will be worst than other. Some trials will try you to the extent of your patience. That is exactly when you need to hold on.

Help is on the way. God already sees your condition and the situation you are facing. Your enemy may not see it but your help sees all things and knows all things. Your enemy can not even hide a secret from God. Every plot, every calculated misdeed, every hated thought, every category of evil that the enemy has is revealed by God.

He will give you joy if you feel like you have lost it all. God gives it to us and it is so powerful. I believe the joy also includes healing. We are healed by His stripes. Can you imagine how the ten lepers felt when they met Jesus? The scripture says that nine walked away while the one stayed to rejoice to thank Jesus. He showed the sign of unspeakable joy. You see, Leprosy was an incurable disease. Nothing could heal this disease. People who had Leprosy were put away into caves and left to die. They were not loved but instead, they hated for no fault of their own. You see why is so good to know Jesus because He will not let you down. He looks at a Leprosy condition and heals you.

CHAPTER 35

TRUE WORSHIP

John 4

REVERSE: GOD WANT S TRUE WORSHIP FROM ALL THAT CALL ON HIS NAME

The Lord our God draws our utmost attention in this life and the life to come simply because of who He is. There is power in worshipping God. I believe that whatever draws you is where you focus your time and energy on. It can be also where and who you worship. Then that source of work and commitment can channel a worship attitude.

In John 4:23-24 Jesus says, But the hour is coming, and now is, when the true worshipers will worship the Father in Spirit and in truth; for the Father is seeking such to worship Him. God is Spirit, and those who worship Him must worship in spirit and truth.

A true worship worships in spirit and truth. He or she follows God. This worship He speaks of is worship that involves a spiritual worship, not our human sides, not dramatic, emotions that involve flesh. But our inner spirit that connects with Him should aim to please God by truth. Our outward worship is a result of the inward worship. People see you on the outside while God sees both and is pleased when he sees the inner worship of man in spirit and truth. The outside can easily be deceptive so He wants the inner man and woman to worship.

Worshiping God allows us to receive a breakthrough. Worshipping God helps in our enter being because we connect solely with the Lord himself. It is direct communication with God almighty. He acknowledges our worship because the worship is strictly for Him. Worshipping our Lord is one of God's absolute commands. But He makes so clear that we must worship in spirit and in truth. That tells me that the Lord's spirit must be inside you to agree in worship. Otherwise you are worshipping a false god referred to as idols.

When I was growing up I never knew that, I always felt something inside me telling me that there was a higher being and connection. It does just happen. The Holy Spirit delivers and directs us to Him. In part of the scripture of John 4, Jesus told the woman at the well that If you knew the gift of God.

Another time in moment is when Jesus was riding upon a donkey that never been rode before. He enters in to Jerusalem and the crowd shouted Hosanna blessed be the one who comes in the name of the Lord. It just so happens to be a song that I love to sing it is called Hosanna blessed be the Rock, blessed be the Rock of my salvation. The people were expecting a King on a stallion in Kings appearance.

Revelation 4: 1-4 after these things I looked, and behold, a door standing open in heaven. And the first voice, which I heard, was like a trumpet speaking with me saying. Come up here
And I will show you things that must take place after this. Immediately I was in the Spirit; and behold, a throne set in heaven, and one sat on the throne. And He who sat on their was like a jasper and a sardius stone in appearance; and there was a rainbow around the throne, in appearance like an emerald. Around the throne were twenty-four thrones, and on the thrones I saw twenty-four elders sitting, clothed in white robes; and they had crowns of gold on their heads.

Revelation 4:5 and from the throne proceeded lightning's, thundering, and voices. Seven lamps of fire were burning before the throne, which are the seven Spirits of God.

Hebrew 8:1 now this is the main point of the things were saying: we have such a High Priest, who is seated at the right hand of the throne of the Majesty in the heavens.

Jesus is our High Priest. God made Him the High Priest because no one could handle this mission but Him.

Hebrew 9: 1-11 When we think of God's blessings we also remember how he set things in order of worship. God shows us His Tabernacle. He explains the order of entering into His presence. What a thought that God would take out the time to explain the order of entering into His presence to worship Him. In the Tabernacle there are seven items in the Holy of Holies. But before you get there, you must understand the set up on the outer court and the inner courts and the requirements to enter.

Who we worship matters more than our diets and our ceremonies, is what the Apostle Paul says. He says not to criticize Christians in their worship and traditions. Everyone is different. We should understand that God knows and sees all things.

Rev 7:9-12 After these things I looked, and behold, a great multitude which no one could number, of all nations, tribes, peoples, and tongues, standing before the throne and before the Lamb, clothed with white robes, with palm branches in their hands, and crying out with a loud voice, saying Salvation belongs to our God who sits on the throne, and to the Lamb!" All the angels stood around the throne and the elders and the four living creatures, and fell on their faces before the throne and worshipped God, saying: Amen! Blessing and glory and wisdom, Thanksgiving and honor and power and might, Be to our God forever and ever. Amen."

CHAPTER 36

PRAISE GOD WITH ALL YOUR MIGHT

Psalm 100 and 34

PSALM 100:1-5 Make a joyful noise unto the LORD, all ye lands. Serve the LORD with gladness: come before his presence with singing. Know ye that the LORD he is God: it is he that hath made us, and not we ourselves; we are his people, and the sheep of his pasture. Enter into his gates with thanksgiving, and into his courts with praise: be thankful unto him, and bless his name. For the LORD is good; his mercy is everlasting; and his truth endureth to all generations.

REVERSE: GOD WANTS HIS PEOPLE TO PRAISE HIM WITH YOUR BEST PRAISE.

We have the rights and the ability to praise God in new song and old song. More importantly with the songs that Holy Spirit gives you in your heart. I believe that there will be days when all the music artists from the most famous to the ones that have not been acknowledged producers, will lift up holy hands and praise Him with all their heart. New songs will be written.

New generations of artist will move in new melodies to magnify and exalt His Holy name. Sing to Jesus the songs of praise and let us exalt Him together. Remember the choir in your church. Remember how you felt when praises went up and blessings came down. It never changed blessings still come down. You can ask King David all about it.

2 Samuel 16:23 and so it was, whenever the spirit from God was upon Saul, that David would take a harp and play it with his hand. Then Saul would become refreshed and well, and the distressing spirit would depart from him.

Before David became King, he was summoned to visit King Saul. Saul had heard that there was a young man who had the spirit of God in him. And he also played music that touched your soul and spirit man. David played a harp which is an instrument for the praise to God. The powerful thing about the harp is that it warded off evil spirits. Saul was relieved of evil spirit by a harp player. The point is that God uses so many types of instruments and people to praise Him. Today we have a man that plays a harp who comes on frequent to the Oprah Winfrey show and Black Entertainment and MTV to display his talent in praising God. I believe all instruments were used to praise His Holy name. I believe that every choir and symphony was gathered on earth to replicate what is happening in heaven. God our father must be praised with the lips and voices of all His creation.

David made a significant statement when he pretended madness before Abimelech, who drove him away, and he departed. *Psalms 34: 1-2 says I will bless the Lord at all times; His praise shall continually be in my mouth.*

Our Lord God wants us to praise Him at all times through the rough times and the good times. We should never stop praising him in those moments because He alone deserves the praise and He allows us to go through things in our live to be tested and I believe it is for our good to go through.

When we praise God he hears us. When we do not praise God there is emptiness. He does not wonder why you are not praising him because He already knows. He knew why David made such a strong effort in his heart of praise to God. David knew when trouble when in the way it was time to praise God. He also knew that God had delivered him many times.

David had many things to praise God about. He had committed adultery. He had a man killed by sending to the front line in the heat of battle. He had a son who wanted to kill him and take his kingdom and authority. When God rescued from these types of situations, you have to praise him. David had many wives and many children. He was a blessed man. It is important to know that we should bless the Lord at all times through the bad times as well as the good times.

2 Samuel 19 And it was told Joab, Behold, the king weepeth and mourneth for Absalom. And the victory that day was turned into mourning unto all the people: for the people heard say that day how the king was grieved for his son. Joab begins to speak to David about his son Absalom whom David's Army had killed. The King cried for days. Sometime after the crying and God wiping away the tears, I believe David came back to himself and learned that God has to be praised. After all it was his life that God was protecting for God glory.

Praise helps unlock the heart. All the chambers, vessels and the entire makeup of the heart is open to magnify God because the spirit of God is inside your heart. That is why we can praise him with all of our heart. It is the very place that keeps life in us. We should be thankful that

God allows us to praise Him from the very place He has life flowing from. What a mighty God we serve. The song writer said angels bow before Him. Heaven and earth adore Him, what a mighty God we serve.

Psalms 8: 1-3. O LORD, our Lord, How excellent is Your name in all the earth, Who have set Your glory above the heavens! Out of the mouth of babes and nursing infants You have ordained strength, Because of Your enemies the enemy and the avenger.

Revelations 19: 5-7 Then a voice came from the throne, saying Praise our God, all you His servants and those who fear Him, both small and great! And I heard, as it were, the voice of a great multitude, as the sound of many waters and as the sound of mighty thundering, saying "Alleluia! For the Lord God Omnipotent reigns! Let us be glad and rejoice and give Him glory, for the marriage of the Lamb has come, and His wife has made herself ready.

Revelation 19:8-9 And to her it was granted to be arrayed in fine linen, clean and bright, for the fine linen is the righteousness acts of the saints. Then he said to me, write blessed are those who are called to the marriage supper of the Lamb! And he said to me, these are the true sayings of God.

A worship and praise experience is always needed to reflect the goodness of God.

Psalm 145: 10-12. All Your work shall praise you, O Lord, And Your saints shall bless you. They shall speak of the glory of your kingdom, and talk of your power, to make known to the sons of men his mighty acts, and the glorious majesty of His kingdom.

I believe our voices of praise do so many things for the now and the future. Today our society and music industry has sang songs and played instrument. One man sings the 23 Psalm while another brother plays the harp like David's harp. Still today it soothes the soul. Still today it soothes the heart of man. And still today it brings healing and restoration and refreshing to all people who know of His goodness. This praise even touches as a witness and a testimony to who God is in our lives.

I believe in the midst of all the trouble David went through especially having to have to live up to being a King, he had to thank God for everything and every experience. Thanks God or demonstrating thanksgiving because so many blessings in our lives. We must surrender to God thanksgiving from the heart. If you can just think for a moment of all the blessing God gave you, could you thank Him. Psalm 106:1-3 Oh, give thanks to the Lord, for He is good. For His mercy endures forever. Who can utter the mighty acts of the Lord? Who can declare all His praise? Blessed are those who keep justice, and he who does righteousness at all times! Remember me, O Lord, with the favor you have toward Your people.

REVERSE THE TIDE

We should thank God our Lord for this life we have. Because when it is gone, it's gone. You can not turn back the clock. You can make all the requests but everything is up to God the Father

Luke 22:30: that you may eat and drink at my table in my kingdom, and sit on thrones judging the twelve tribes of Israel.

CHAPTER 37

ACTIVATE YOUR GOD GIVEN GIFTS

Ephesians 4:11, 1 Corinthians 12, Romans 12

REVERSE: ACCEPT YOUR GIFTS. USE YOUR GIFT FOR THE GLORY OF GOD AND HIS KINGDOM. BE FILLED WITH GIFTS AND OVERFLOWING JOY FOR GOD'S SERVICE.

We are gifted people by the Holy Spirit because He has given them to us and we accept them. God made every gift available for His chosen people. These gifts are given to be ministered to the body of Jesus Christ. Some people have more than one gift, nevertheless these gifts are not superior to the other gift. The purpose of these gifts are to to build up the body of Christ and to minister to people. They are used to unify the body of Christ and strengthen people in the ministry. When God give gifts we are not to be puffed up with our spiritual gifts. In the Corinthian Church, people with gifts started personal rivalries between others with gifts. Using gifts improper can lead to confusion and splits in the church. This occurred in the Corinthian church because people were out of order and started using them for personal gain and attention during church services. One major point in using gifts is to avoid manipulating others with your gift. Your gift is your gift to be used. However, it is the Holy Spirit who causes the change and transformation in people. He can use you in His works. In verse one He does not want us to be ignorant of these gifts. If you use your gift for self gain, you may become devisive causing the church to divide, while these gifts are used to edify the Lord and strengthen the Church. This means Jesus is expecting these gifts to exalt Him. Verse 7 explains that every man will profit from these gifts. Vs3 explains that Christians must have discernment and apply a test to determine if a person is a false prophet or not. There are nine gifts in 1 Corinthians 12: According to *Dobson, et al.,(1994)* The Spirit of

Wisdom has to do with speech that consist wisdom as the primary composition and content. Wisdom helps in explaining right and wrong, discernment. Wisdom gives information leading a person onto the right side. The word of knowledge is deals with truth and is associated with the previous gifts. This is associated with the personal knowledge of God. The Holy Spirit reveal knowledge in the form of truthRevelation knowledge is God speaking directly from Heaven to Saints. The gift of faith is the kind of faith that move mountains. This kind of faith works wonders in the lives of Saints. This faith allows us to become dependent and trust in in the Holy Spirit to work in our lives. Healing is delivering someone from a sickness one example is a disease such as Jesus did with healing Lepers. Healing refers to the fact that a special gifts occurs at each healing. This gift emphasizes the process of healing. Divine healing occurs with the gift of healing. The gift of Miracles are witnessing something similar to Jesus turning water into wine. Miracles are associated with the event in Acts 5:1-12. Another example is Acts 9:32-40. Peter excersized the gift. It is a demonstration of Jesus supernatural power as well raising Lazarus from the dead. The gift of Prophecy is for-telling the future; Prophecy is also special revelation from God in which special messages come from God in heaven. Prophecy is also preaching the gospel; Prophecy is associated with Acts 11:28. The majority of the New Testament epistle are referenced of prophecy. Discerning is the gift of distinguishing true prophets from false prophets. 1 John 4:1 is what John had in mind referencing discernment; A person with this gift can discern if a another person is speaking for God or speaking by an evil spirit; It is distinguishing between and recognize. Tongues is the gift to speak in a language not understood by the speaker According to *Dobson, et al.,(1994)* Tongues was limited to speaking in known languages (Acts 2:4). He says since this is the case the interpretation of Tongues was vital in every instance. Tongues is communicating to God in a mystery. Divers kind of tongues means different kinds of tongues; Interpretation of Tongues means a person has a gift to explain what is spoken in the Church. God divide these gifts as He will by the same Spirit *(Dobson, et al.,1994).*

Dobson et.al (1994) reminds the reader that all of these gifts come from one Spirit, our Lord God. They are diverse gifts but God is the source of power *(Dobson, et al., 1994).*

CHAPTER 38

THE MOVE OF GOD

JUDGES 7

GOD WANTS US TO MOVE WHEN HE CALLS

REVERSE: THE MOVE OF GOD IS ALWAYS AN ANNOITED MOVE TO GLORIFY GOD. WHEN HE SETS SOMETHING IN MOTION, IT WILL NOT FELL. GIDEON MOVED IN OBEDIENCE WHEN GOD SID MOVE.

The first time you walked on your job and the weeks to come your boss or supervisor told you to do several things that required moving. What are you going to do when God ask you to move for Him? God does not need help moving neither in our life nor with anything. He is the God who orchestrates all existence and movements. If you just wonder about the space frontier, it's God who moves it and makes it evolve. Before you or I could imagine, He already knows. Nothing can escape Him. He can see all and He hears all and He moves in those that love Him and He is also available for those who are lost. God moves in the lives of many people so mysteriously, yet demonstrating His awesome authority and power. God used a man by the name of Gideon and He used Him in tremendous ways. Gideon was one of God's chosen men to go to battle against the Midianites. Gideon had the kind of heart that God was looking for to do His mission. He was about to embark on a task only a few could follow under obedience. God deals with huge armies. In this instance, He gave Gideon an army of men and tested their faith before the battle and during the battle.

Judges 7:7 Then the Lord said to Gideon, by the three hundred men who lapped I will save you, and deliver the Midianites into your hand, Let all the other people go, every man to his place.

We watch things on a daily basis especially specific television programs with their sitcoms and movie series, and other athletic broadcasts. But what sparked me one day are the movies on big screens now a days. Animation and advanced technology is doing wonders for the industry. A movie that made millions topping the box office was called 300. It was amazing to see such a movie that could make money so fast with visual effects. But one day a family member asked me could we watch the movie together as a family. As I begin to watch the movie, we suddenly came up on a scene involving intimacy and of course I had to stop it and try to fast forward it. So we did and the movie came to a climax and it dawned on me that these 300 men that fought Armies galore had a certain battle technique. They fought as a unit against any size enemy and defeated them. It dawned on me while the movie was playing that God had touched the filmmaker in a way that even the filmmaker had not realized. The movie was really a reflection of the type army God gave to Gideon. These men had to have a heart of courage that reflected the might of God almighty. When Gideon's army fought nothing was left. He did not do like Saul. He eliminated everything. The significance of Gideon is that he trusted in the living God to conquer in battle with a few good men that trust God Judges 7:19-22

CHAPTER 39

CROSSOVER BARRIERS

REVERSE: LORD HELP ME TO CROSS OVER FROM HELL TO
SALVATION. DO NOT LET ANYTHING OR ANYONE STOP
YOU. YOU NEED JESUS NOW.

*LUKE 16:19 There was a certain rich man who was clothed in purple
and fine linen and fared sumptuously every day. But there was a
certain beggar named Lazarus, full of sores who was laid at his gate,
desiring to be fed with the crumbs which fell from the rich man's
table. Moreover the dogs came and licked his sores. So it was that the
beggar died, and was carried by the angels to Abraham's bosom. The
rich man also died and was buried. And being in torments in Hades,
he lifted up his eyes and saw Abraham afar off, and Lazarus in his
bosom. Then he cried and said, Father Abraham, have mercy on me,
and send Lazarus that he may dip the tip of his finger in water and
cool my tongue; for I am tormented in this flame.*

Our lives can go up into a flame or like a puff of smoke in a
moment if we disregard aligning ourselves with the King of Glory,
Jesus Christ our Lord. Barriers exist to stop people from moving in
the right direction in life. Barriers are constructed and put in place to
bring something to a halt, confusion, stop a task or mission, or even
making you quit. Barriers can make you lose confidence, make wrong
decisions. God wants to see if you will maneuver and crossover those
barriers in your life. There are drugs used as a barrier, sex trafficking,
alcoholism, lust, jealousy, pride, envy and idolatry and even adultery.
All of these can be barriers that keep you from seeking God and
getting a breakthrough in life. Those are the kind of things that send
people where the rich man ended up.

If we align ourselves we can get a glimpse of heaven even when
hell is chasing us and you feel captured by the enemy. God's power
and will can do anything but fail. It takes faith to experience God's

power and will. At the same time, God's will and power is already activated. Lazarus attitude took him into the bosom of Abraham which is in the presence of God in heaven, the Lord's dwelling place. The rich man's attitude took him to a place where there is continuous torment. Hell is that place. Hell is the place to simply avoid with all my strength. When we think about where we really do not want our souls to end up. The thought of hell should really give a reality check and open our minds and drive people to make the best decision of life.

That decision is to ask Jesus for forgiveness and ask Jesus to come into your heart and make you a new creature in Christ Jesus. Lazarus had a good spirit. He was meek and lowly. God recognized that and placed him in Abraham's bosom so that the rich man could see from hell and tell of the thirst that he desires. God is the thirst quencher. He can give living water anytime and anywhere. So he could also testify through the portal of seeing through Hell to Heaven. Such a thing that only God could do for His own purpose and Glory. We all want to cross over to the other side because all blessings are on that side with Jesus our Lord. That side is Kingdom of God. We must be born of God and must have that relationship that makes us humble ourselves before God almighty and set the light of God to show the world of His goodness and mercy.

God has warned many people that there will be a time when it's too late. We as saints of the Most High God have an obligation to all that have not accepted Jesus as Lord and Savior of their life. Crossing over into the Kingdom of God will set a new order in your life. Keep in mind what you have done when you accept Jesus. It means the old man is gone and the new man is alive. Crossing over means that you have just enlisted into the Army of God.

I thought about the power of His overflow in my life. He love that overflows in my life And His blessings that overflow in my life. His abundant rain tells the story in my life and in the life of His people. Not only does He bless us in the abundant areas of life, He keeps on sending more and more of His love that we may know Him intimately and in the fullness of His Spirit.

What was brought to my attention as blessing is that God showers us with rain because God is in the business of replenishing the earth and the substance that man is in need of for survivability and sustainment. Just like God pours the water on your house and washes your house, He also pours the water to feed the cattle on a thousand hills. He also pours the water to nourish the crop for farmers who have experienced a drought and need to be successful in that trade. God always has a way of blessings us when we see things the opposite of how He has planned for us.

I want to remind us of what God said in His word. There is a latter rain. God is saying let it rain because you will experience prosperity. Let the rain blanket me, cover me in the fullest of blessings. He wants us to experience the rain because the rain is an expression of abundance. All over the world crops and people who were thirsty received the power of filling a quenching thirst. People are tired of feeling the dryness and emptiness in their lives. God has a way of allowing us to know that the rain is symbolic of blessings flowing in our lives. Rain signifies that there will be some fruit that will get watered. There are some fruit that has be stable and stagnant and burdened because it has not be nourished by essential nutrients.

For so many people, it will take the rain to remove the scales from their eyes. When this rain touches you, you will surely be blessed in the Lord. This rain will wash away conditions that keep you tied down in bondage. This rain has spiritual power. You want to get Jesus no matter what the issue was and still seems to be your life. Make Him the living water in your life. The scripture says, he will flow like rivers of water in your belly.

In Joel 2, he says, I will pour out my Spirit. Well, He will pour out His Spirit in more intensity than the rain that flows down and runs off of your back when your are soak and wet. Ask God to do an outpouring of the Spirit in your life and start a new walk in Christ. Start a new tongue. Start the fivefold ministry gifts that you have possessed. Watch it come to pass. I tell you that God has such a down pour of ministry that exist that we as Christians all over the world can not keep up. You want to start ministering. It is available 24/7. He will equip you.

CHAPTER 40

GOD'S TIME

REVERSE: GOD WANTS YOUR SEASON AND TIME TO BE
UNDER HIS CONTROL. YOU ARE ON GOD'S TIME.

TIME AND SEASON

*Ecclesiastes 3:1-8 To everything there is a season, A time for every
purpose under heaven: A time to be born, And a time to die; A time to
plant, And a time to pluck what is planted; A time to kill; And a time to
heal;*

This is your season to submit yourself to God. No longer will you
turn your back on God when he called you out of the abyss. This
simply means God was calling you out of darkness as time went by
and you knew that you needed to get Jesus in your life after living in
pure hell and nightmares Although God is the controller of time and
seasons, he allows us to make a choice. He made time for His purpose.
He controls and will not let it go. You can count on that! You and I are
on God's time. Have you ever heard someone say that to you? People
who get paid by the hour when they are fixing your sink or repairing
your roof or even doing some office work for you will tell you that
they are on the clock and cannot afford to lose out on the pay. It
simply means pay up or I have to go. We thank God that he does not
force his hand like men do. Imagine if we had to pay God as though he
was on the clock. You and I would need two or three jobs just to keep
up with payments. Really we can never repay Jesus for His work on
cavalry. Wherever you are at this very moment in time, you need to
know that only God knows and can monitor you. You cannot hide
anywhere or at any time. When prophets exercise their gifts of
prophesying or giving prophecy about specific events, a true prophet
that is receives it from God only and not of his or her own power.
Prediction of the future involves time, wisdom, revelation and the

174

word from God. Since God was already here dwelling where He desire do to dwell, He could make time and use it for His purpose. One of the most important parts of time is the time to heal wounds and scars. Somehow it works almost every time.

Believers know that God has the power to controls everything from heaven and any place that He wants to control. He owns an operation center everywhere, in every country, in every nation, in every city, in every state, in every house and in ever temple, every Church, and on every mission. No one can stop Him from controlling all things. That right, He controls the waters, the skies, the valleys, the rivers, the oceans, man, woman, children, spiritual things light, darkness, life on earth, everlasting life and all things in the imagination and beyond it. We still need to understand that God alone created all things:

In GENESIS 1:1-10, God reveals to us, "In the beginning God created the heavens and the earth. The earth was without form, and void; and darkness was on the face of the deep. And the Spirit of God was hovering over the face of the waters. Then God said, "Let there be light"; and there was light. And God saw the light that it was good; and God divided the light from the darkness. God called the light Day, and the darkness He called Night. So the evening and the morning were the first day. Then God said, "Let there be a firmament in the midst of the waters, and let it divide the waters from the waters." Thus God made the firmament, and divided the waters which were under the firmament from the waters which were above the firmament; and it was so. And God called the firmament Heaven. So the evening and the morning were the second day. Then God said, "Let the waters under the heavens be gathered together into one place, and let the dry land appear"; and it was so. And God called the dry land Earth, and the gathering together of the waters He called Seas. And God saw that it was good.

It is a blessing when you know that this rain is coming from heaven. It is God who sends the rain for the earth and the welfare of people. It good that God gives us the waters in the seas and oceans and all through the land. He blesses us with the abundance of rain.

CHAPTER 41

GOD'S AUTHORITY

MATTHEW 8

MATTHEW 8:8-9 The Centurion answered and said, Lord I am not worthy that You should come under my roof. You should come under my roof. But only speak a word and my servant will b healed. For I am a man under authority, having soldiers und me. And I say to this one, Go and he goes; and to another, come and he comes and to my servant Do this and he does it.

A tough and rugged soldiers stands in the presence of Jesus and allows his faith to be known. This centurion soldier reminds me that there are many soldiers like him today with faith that welcomes the power of God to work in their lives. However, there are some soldiers that allow the enemy to tell them other stories tend to stay away. That is not what Jesus wants from Christian soldiers and those in the United States Armed Forces. There are Centurion kind of soldiers in the Army, Air Force, Marines, Navy and all forces throughout the world. God wants all Soldiers to know about His authority. God's authority is higher than all the Presidents and generals and every soldier put together

JOHN 5:24-27 Most assuredly, I say to you, he who hears My word and believes in Him who sent Me has everlasting life, and shall not come into judgment, but has passed from death into life. Most assuredly, I say to you, the hour is coming, and now is, when the dead will hear the voice of the Son of God; and those who hear will live. For as the Father has life in Himself; so He has granted the Son to have life in Himself. And has given Him authority to execute judgment also, because He is the Son of Man.

CHAPTER 42

THE WILL OF GOD FOR YOUR LIFE

Matthew 26:39 He went a little farther and fell on His face, and prayed, saying " O My Father, If it is possible, let this cup pass from Me; nevertheless, not as I will but as You will"

It is powerful that Jesus used the word will to His Father. He used it because everything was about the Fathers will. Jesus understood, although asking if it be possible to let the cup pass from Him, that it was the Father's will. Jesus wanted to glorify His Father so He did what God sent Him to do, die for our sins. What is the will of God for your life? You need to commune with Jesus Christ and He will give you more answers. The will of God for your life is to serve Him wholeheartedly without interruptions. The will of God for your life is to be an example like Jesus Christ in whatever fashion and how God directs you. His will for you life is to take on the mind of Christ. His will for you life is that no one perish but live with the inheritance that is laid up for you. God gives out other things concerning his will day and night. You want to know the will of God for your life, then start walking in obedience and worship Him. You discover the will of God for your life when you have a personal relationship. Start living a God centered life so you will be directed like Noah was to build and Ark. He fell right into God's will for his life and it affected his family and the entire world. Read Genesis 6

Walking in the will of God is our purpose on earth. His will is embedded into our lives whether we want to accept it or not. The fact remains that there is a God and no one like Him who controls all things because He created all things. You want your life anchored in His will no matter what the cost. His will is the vital step in our lives. We have our own individual will. That will also has a form of power but it is not the same will of God. It is limited in what it can do because it is based on our natural abilities and intellect. When we face the hardest problem in life, we depend on the will inside of us. If it is your will of it will fail, if it is the will of God it will succeed because He can never fail. In the passage, Jesus displayed in my mind the strongest and most remarkable. This has the be one of the most controversial subjects because people wonder why God has all of that will but allowed His son to be crucified. He separated Himself from His son for a moment. He did what he had to do to destroy the sting of death and all of the demonic spirits and captivity.

HE WILL DESCEND FROM HEAVEN

2 Thessalonians 4:16-17. For the Lord Himself will descend from heaven with a shout, with the voice of an archangel, and with the trumpet of God, And the dead in Christ will rise first. Vs. Then we who are alive and remain shall be caught up together with them in the clouds to meet the Lord in the air, and thus we shall always be with the lord.

Make life count now is the best thing for any Christian or anyone who believes that one day they will make a decision to Christ. Pursue Jesus with all of your might because something will always try to stop you in your tracks. I will never forget the sermon I had to preach. The Preacher of the house had made a statement to me, Preach man! I never felt so confident in knowing that people were behind me in the preaching. But there was a different side after the sermon. Sometimes we learn from the very people that did not inspire us to aspire in the ministry. What it does for me is remind me of my calling and His many blessings that are in store for me. It also reminds me of knowing that I am in His will in his plan of life. Everyone should take on a hot pursuit attitude to know that when He returns that you will be caught up in His will. This will help us to be caught up in the air when He returns.

Please understand if it was not for His death on the cross, we would not have to expect the a return. In John 19:30 So when Jesus had received the sour wine, He said, it is finished! And bowing His head, He gave up His spirit. This is the blessing of taking away the sin of the world. We were saved by Jesus taking on all of our punishment.

178

You see the blessing never stops because of His everlasting love.

HE DIED FOR ME!

John 19:33-34 But when they came to Jesus and saw that He was already dead, they did not break His legs. But one of the soldiers pierced His side with a spear, and immediately blood and water came out. The only reason people live today like me and you is because He blessed us in His death. You have a life right now because of Him. No one else could do this for you. What greater love than this that a man lay down His life. In return love Him back with all you heart, mind, soul and strength. All praise, blessings, honor and glory to His Holy name.

CHAPTER 43

THE POWER THAT HEAL

Luke 17:12-16 then as he entered a certain village, there met Him ten men who were lepers, who stood afar off. And they lifted up their voices and said, Jesus, Master, have mercy on us! So when He saw them, He said to them, go show yourselves to the priests. And so it was that as they went, they were cleansed.

Reverse The Tide: Only the power of God can heal. Ask Him today to heal your situation and believe.

The kind of cleansing power that Jesus offers daily is the power that heals people. Jesus unleashes His power everyday when we call upon Him for help. Cast your care upon Him (1Peter5:7). He will answer your prayer. In Luke 17, One of the Lepers that Jesus healed came back and praised God with a loud voice. To be cleansed in the flesh is easy. You can just use soap and water in many ways. However, to be cleaned from disease, suffering and sin, we need Jesus' power applied to our situation. Most people seek out a physician who prescribe the best medicine, that is fine but we need Jesus in every situation to guide the physician as well. Jesus is our physician with power. All of His prescriptions will work. These Lepers described in this story had a healing experience with Jesus Christ Himself. We all need the Holy Spirit who will heal us according to the perfect will of God. This type of cleansing took power to changed sick men into whole men. It was a cleansing that would be memorable for years to come. The leper that came back acknowledged the miracle healing power of the Lord. This man was appreciative in a personal way, persuaded, and passionate about what Jesus had done in His life. Have you ever displayed that kind of attitude toward our Lord and Savior for the healing He has done or what He is about to do in your life. Christians and all people should show God that they are thankful with the spirit of exalting His Holy name.

Philippians 3:12-14

SPIRIT FILLED

God sees the blood flowing in a perfect cycle or system of flowing. God sees the blood in man's body as His perfect substance as He places man in a perfect position for life. Again it has the perfect cycle by God's creative design. God even makes the blood flow in a perfect cycle even when there are crisis in our lives. My testimony is that God worked on my family members behalf. Someone had to be carrier of cycle cell trait to make it extend in the family line. I never forget the day the doctor told me so many years ago not to marry another carrier. If you connect with another carrier then sickle cell trait could become full blown sickle cell anemia, which means to most doctors tragedy approaching. Please keep in mind the God we serve. The testimony is that God helped my daughter through her sickle cell crisis while she had been pregnant. Through all the medicine and pain and irritations and upsets and backsets, a miracle happened. Several weeks later a baby by the name of Faith Divine was born, Oct 2, 2007. She was 5.15 pounds and 18 inches long with jet black hair, kicking and screaming indicating that she had healthy lungs. I believe she is a delight in God's eye and in the family's as well. The most important thing is that she was healthy. God is still in the blessing business. What an awesome God we serve. It is a testament to the power of His love and His blessings in our lives. The primary point here is that God is a healing God in the midst of what seems to keep you down.

CRIPLE OR LAME - BLESSED THROUGH DISABILITIES

God is always blessings people. In the militaries all around the world, wars have impacted the lives of people. Some have lost limbs because of heroic acts of valor. Some have lost limbs because of deadly flesh eating diseases and other reasons such as car accidents and more. God wants us to deliver the message to all of the people affected that He loves you and your life is not over. In fact, God is going to get you up and you can have joy and laugh it off and tell the devil go back to hell! God said take your dirty hands off me. I am blessed and highly favored. To you it may not look like it but I am. I was watching a man on television preach with no arms and no legs. That is at the top of the list of most amazing things I ever saw in my life. He could have just laid down and been defeated and just died off. Instead he found Jesus Christ and started running faster than people that have legs and arms. His witness touches the world. My friend. God can use you right now! Today! Give your life to Jesus right now! Repeat this, Father I repent of my sin, I believe that you died on the cross and was buried, then rose from the dead with all power. Say this, I accept you as Lord and Savoir in my heart. You are born again. When you go to church, you can stand before the congregation and do it publicly so witnesses have seen the evidence of the power of God in your life. Do it. Help us reverse lives of those have been scared, injured and lost, beat up and running from Jesus Christ.

Another powerful story in the Bible is the story of Maphiboseth. Maphiboseth was the grandson of Saul. He was injured by being dropped as a baby. So that made him a cripple all of his life. As the story has it. He was left for dead until David found him on a road. He saw himself as a nobody. He was ready to die and give up hope. He felt no hope in healing. He felt no hope in family and friends. But the blessing is on the way. He received blessings from David because David found favor in him because he was of the house of Saul. David made it plain that Maphiboseth would sit at his table and feast from this day on. One main point here is that you have the ability to restore in person by the blessings of God, do it before it is too late. Do it because God already blessed you. Do it because the love of God is shed abroad in our hearts and minds. Do it because you honor God. Bless people who have any condition with your heart.

Still thinking of His blessing and power to shower us on earth with rain. I continued watching this same rain that comes from above come down on my roof, I observed the overflow of the water in my gutters, I was a little concerned for a moment because there should have been a perfect flow from the gutters to the down spout then to the ground. I thought something was going to get backed up and find a crack or an opening to get into and create a devastating leak in my house. When it rains that hard (thunders shower), you definitely want to have a good roof and water flow. If the roof leaks there is potential for something in your house to cave in and get destroyed. Things do get expensive and inconvenient.

CHAPTER 44

THE POWER OF GOD'S LOVE

1 Corinthians 13:1 though I speak with the tongues of men and of angels, but have not love, I have become sounding brass or clanging symbols.

Reverse the Tide: Love reverse family and relationship situations. You must apply love daily in all situations when needed. Don't just say it, live it

The most powerful force in the Bible is God's love. There are several types of love. Phileo love is natural affection and spontaneous love. Phileo love is defines as being a friend to someone. Another type of love is the Greek work Agapa. Agapa love is unconditional love. Agapa love cannot be earned. Agapa love is given when a person is undeserving. Love is given regardless of circumstances. God expresses Agape love in Corinthians 13. The Bible clearly tells us that the Love of God is shed abroad in our hearts and minds by the Holy Ghost. God cares a great deal that we speak in tongues because it is a gift offered to God's people. Through the Apostle Paul, God express that if we speak in tongues and do not have love, our witness really has issues with others. Speaking tongues is not more powerful than expressing the love of God to others. Love is the key to healing. Love is the key to helping. Love is the key to making people feel better about them. Love is the key to having a personal relationship with God. Love is the key to have a strong marriage. Love is the Key to helping friends get through rough times. Love is also the key to helping other people get through rough times.

Love has a way of helping you recover through hard times and difficult breakups, heart aches and brokenness. In 1 Corinthians 13, the Apostle Paul reminds that love is stronger than all of those things that come against us and put us in another frame of mind. He even reminds that love never gives up on you. Love is greater than hope and faith. It does not boast. Love is not puffed up. Love restores. Love makes life better. Love in Who Jesus is in 1 John 4. Love changes lives of people when they go through love that was lost. Love can save a marriage that was on the rocks and on the verge of divorce. Love is more powerful that being showered in the rain. Love cleans up the heart. King David asked God to create in him a clean heart and renew a right spirit in him. It is the love of God that can hear the heart of repentance and wash sin away and forgive. Love never fails because God is love and God cannot fail. Love makes you smile. Love renews relationships among all family members and no one is left out. Love brings husbands and wives back together. Love brings siblings together. Love lifts up families and brings family reunions. Love removes scars that have been in your heart and mind for years. The power of God's love is always expressed even in the atmosphere. The power of God's love is what raised Jesus from the dead. He can raise your life up from a dead state and things that hold you down like issues of life, bondages and hate. The love of God is shed abroad in our hearts and minds by the power of the Holy Spirit. God demonstrated His love and His continues to reveal love. In *John 3:16-17 For God so loved the world that He gave His only begotten Son, that whosoever believes in Him should perish but have everlasting life. For God did not send His Son into the world to condemn the world, but that the world through Him might be saved.*

The Lord wants us to love Him back: *Matthew 22:26 Love the Lord with all your heart mind and soul and strength,*

I am reminded of a situation in Kansas when a beggar came up to me and asked the simple question will you buy me a sandwich. Of course you wonder why he stands there asking everyone that comes by. It is because those that he asked they do exactly what I am saying they come by. So the beggar or poor man is just asking for $1.50 to purchase a sandwich or drink to eat a meal after missing the last five meals or a year of meals. The point is that we need to show the love in times that really count.

This is why Jesus wants people to love. He came to demonstrate His love through humanity. He gave up the one single son that He had to save people who deserved the wrath of God.

REVERSE DRIVING DRUNK:

Remember Acts 2:38 Jesus wants us to be filled with the Holy Ghost, not with alcohol that taints your mind and makes you go out of control. Those men in Acts were filled with the Holy Ghost to be used by God. I want to tell men today that reverse that kind of driving and put into to gear and reverse and drive for Jesus Christ to let people know of His grace and blessings. Let them know he has unmerited favor awaiting them.

God can reverse your thinking when it comes to drinking and driving. The reversal starts when you say to our Lord Jesus Christ, Lord, I respect and honor you. Therefore I pledge from my heart not to drive intoxicated, drugged nor with any illegal substance or substance that causes harm to me and other people. Drinking and driving sounds so cliché, however, in reality people are still drinking and driving as those they were never told to do so. The message is simple with drinking and driving. First of all, drinking and driving kill's hundreds of people in which many are innocent drivers that have not even had a drink. The drivers that are drinking and driving are causing mass devastation. Do not drink and drive if you care about anyone in your life? No you will not drink and drive because you do care about what Jesus thinks of you. You care about affecting other people.

The Lord makes it clear to all us if we want to be drunk be drunk in the spirit like those men were in the upper room when the Holy Ghost came upon them and they spoke in different languages. Allow Jesus to take the wheels of your life. Accept him in your life today. Do not take another swig of that jungle juice of Hennessey or rum or beer. Do not engage in any drugs that take your mind. All Jesus to take you're your mind and all of you. He is more powerful than all the drugs and alcohol combines. Do you know someone who is an alcoholic behind the wheel of their vehicle and they just will not stop. Approach with love and tell them what Jesus wants to do. He wants to take the wheel for them and guide their lives to salvation and in the Kingdom as servants to fulfill their purpose. Tell them their purpose is to please God and not destroy lives but build other people up in the name of Jesus Christ.

DON'T DRIVE TALKING ON THE CELL PHONE

Did you see the young man who went on television to announce his drunk driver encounter? Not only did he kill an innocent person because he was drinking and talking on the cell phone, he scarred his life and the families are suffering as well.

My friend please put the cell phone up while you are driving. God does not want you to cause a major pile up on the highway or any road. Pray that our Lord reverse my thinking and yours when I have the cell phone to my ear in the car. Stop me in my tracks O' Lord. Driving while talking on cell phones in deep conversation on the phone while driving is no longer something new. It is happening by the thousands. That means thousands and thousands are endangered. Cell phones have taken on a role of itself because people are not acting sensitive to others that are innocent bystanders on the road just going about their own business until that driver who is intoxicated and that driver that is constantly talking on the cell phone and having heated conversation that take their minds off the road. Do you know someone who drives drunk? If so it's your duty to tell them stop in the name of our Lord. Do you know someone who talks on the cell phone while they are driving? It only takes one mistake and you can cause a mass car pileup. This is so important the Oprah Winphrey often speaks on it the subject of driving with cell phones to the nation Cell phones are so important. I stopped by your place today inside this book to let you know that Jesus wants you to talk to him more than you do anyone else. The devil and his demons want you to have a car pile-up with multiple casualties. We rebuke him in the name of Jesus Christ, the Son of the living God. Jesus wants you to take the cell phone down from your ear and sing praises as you talk to him about what your purpose in life is. Do not miss this conversation with Jesus today.

Count of three put the cell phone down in your car especially and take a few minutes to ask Jesus what is your purpose in life. Find that scripture that God tells you about the plan on your life he has for you.

Chapter 1 of the Book of Romans explains what you need to know about living the proper sexual lifestyle Please understand from the start, God loves all of his people. He does not love all the acts of disobedience and things not pleasing in his sight. Homosexuality is not acceptable in God's sight. He made a man and women to get married and reproduce. A man having sex with another man cannot produce. It was never in God's plan. That is why it's not natural as God made sex to be. Even in Sodom and Gomorra the Lord God expressed what he thought about that behavior. He sent brimstone and fire, destroying the entire city. This was because of sexual immorality. He does not love things that he did not set in motion. If it is not of God, then it is more than likely of the evil one. Get from the down Low back up to on top. Get back on with your sexuality lifestyle intact with the God. Sexuality was made by God, not man. You and I did not get to decide anything about our sex makeup when God started us in the womb. God made this very simple. A man is to marry a woman and that is it. Why is it this way? Only a man and woman can produce a child. A man and a man cannot produce a child. A woman and a woman cannot produce a child. God said to Adam and Noah be fruitful and multiply. Even before we get to the scripture, it is instinctively embedded in our DNA, instinctively embedded in our morality. More important, it is in the word of God. Romans Chapter 1 of the Bible keeps it real. That is your reference. Read it so you will be clear on this subject. Remember, you are reading God's word. He is speaking to you plain and clear and in plain sight. Nothing to hide! God still loves all of but he is displeased with acts that are not according to his will.

ADULTROUS SPIRIT (see Galatians 5)

We are talking about reversing the tide. The tide is heavy. The tide is like a hurricane coming your way. Some tides are like temptation. Sexual temptation is strong like a hurricane because lust kicks in and says yes I will do that! She has a tender touch and a smile that will knock you off your feet. I know you did not say anything. But she is over there staring you down sexually and you know you are married brother. In your mind, don't care, got to go! That girl looks to good! What will you do if she approaches you and say, can we hook up? Wow, your dream just came true because you were watching her as well. You did not ask the question are you married.The real deal is that you did not want to know because she did not ask you until it was over. You left your boy and went home with Sherita and spent all night at her house especially after you and her got fully wasted with wine and mixed drinks. Surprise, its not just her house. Her husband came in the middle of your act and half killed you and her. So now what is up? While you guys got in the tussle, you noticed something unusual. Sherita was hiding her self and the components that you thought were girly. In the tussle as you were half way knocked out, you saw a man part of Sherita. After Paul B. tossed you out of the house, you realized that you committed adultery by having sexual relationship with a man. You also realized that you though she was a woman but because you were so drunk, Sherita treated you like a woman sexually and that was your first time so the evidence was your body. Ten days later, you realize that you have herpes. Five months later you discover, Sherita had HIV. Marriage is made for man and woman, not the same sex. Sodom and Gomorrah is one the prime examples that God uses in Genesis because those who want sexual relation as oppose to what God ordain, cause trouble. Because of this act in Sodom, God destroy the entire city with brimstone and fire. He hates homosexual acts. The men had a chance to reverse the tide. They could have made things right with God. When we do not take full advantage of our faith that enables us to reverse things that are ungodly, we insult God.

TORNADO: These huge storms may hit areas without warning and cause serious tragedy. But Our Lord wants us to still hold your head high. Our Lord God is still gracious and loving when we experience the worst of storms. God wants his people to know that he will bless them for all the trouble that they have gone through. You home and family may have experienced a level 4 or 5 worst category tornado, but God will give you double for your trouble. Seek our Lord Jesus Christ for recovery operation and the restorer of your life.

FLOODS: Raging water that has power to destroy property and life. Floods come and go causing damages. However, you can trust God to restore your life. Turn your life over to Jesus Christ. He is your help in times of trouble.

Tsunami- this is a raging storm that causes extreme damage as it has in Asia, New Orleans, and Japan. God's power and love will help you get through it. God's power is more powerful than a tsunami.

DIVORCE- Remain with your Husband. Remain with your wife. Get through difficult times by calling on Jesus for help in your relationship and the tough times. You can weather the storm if you seek God and work together. Ask God for guidance. Keep God the center of your marriage so you will not have to get a divorce.

ABUSE: If you are an abuser, God wants you to stop it now. If you have been abuse, ask the Lord Jesus Christ to heal you from all of those moments of abuse. God will remove it and fill you with His love in your heart and remove the scars and wounds.

RESPECT YOUR HUSBAND: Use the scripture in Ephesians 5. Wives your life is centered on God and He will focus your attention on your husband. A woman whose life is guided by God will respect her husband and never disrespect him. She will honor her husband at all times. She upholds the vows in the marriage. She prays for him and helps him all the time. Disrespect is not in the equation

RESPECT WIFE; Use Ephesian 5. Husbands, your life and the marriage is centered on Jesus Christ. He loves her as himself. He gives her things to bless her. He gives her roses. He gives her his heart to love. He honors her completely. He upholds the vows in the marriage. He prays for his wife. The Husband role is to be a priest in the marriage. He prays for her daily.

RESPECT CHILDREN: Children are to show respect to parents at all times. Children regardless of your age, you must show respect to all adults. If you are in the shopping mall, you show respect, if you are in school you show respect. Your respect starts at home by your parents training you in the Lord and you receiving it honorably. If you respect your parents like God says, your days will be long. Make the Lord Jesus Christ be please with you. Honor Him. Carry your self with respect inward and outward, it means how you dress as well and having a positive and loving attitude.

DIABETIES; God on a diet and defeat the enemy who wants to rob you of your health.

MILITARY MEN AND WOMEN: These are people who stand for freedom and hope, and democracy upheld. Military men and women fight wars against terrorism to maintain freedoms. This are the people who stand guard while other Americans sleep at night in their beds without fear. These are men and women who have been wounded, some with purple hearts and their lives are not the same anymore. They gave the ultimate sacrifice for freedom and are known as heroes.

MENTOR'S PROGRAMS: A mentor is someone who cares for another person and sets the example while volunteering to help a specific person to stay on or get on a progressive path for life. He she is required a background check. A mentor helps a youth or a specific person set priorities and achieve goals that are set by a mentee and his mentor and parents if needed. A mentor helps to guide a person by assessing the attitude and behavior and concerns with family, friends and society. God uses the mentor to disseminate the word of God for encouragement in whatever problem that mentee is experiencing. Your son or daughter might need a mentor. Find a local center so your child can have someone to connect with.

EDUCATION AND PARENTS: Education is available. There is no excuse for not pursuing education. Education is knowledge through public school systems and advance school system through college. Education is formed so people will have knowledge and us it to be successful on jobs. Education is so important African American such as Martin L. King, the worlds great civil rights leader, Frederick

Douglas, Jane Pitman, Row vs. Brown- A education dispute in 1965, Plessy vs. Ferguson school board.

Encouraging People to Life Right In the Eyes of God

Family can reverse the tide in many areas of life.

One of the major concerns in society is that of men. Men of all races need to take back the home. In America, one of the leading problems is that of Black Men abandonment of the child. Black Men need to take back his home. For all men, do not just impregnate a young girl just because you can take advantage. Do not abandon her and the child. You must stand up like a man and take responsibility.

Role Models and Mentors: There are several men that have the ability to be a role model. It is time to step up to the plate and be a role model at home and to other youth. If you want to be a role model, you don't walk around like you portray a thug attitude. If you glorify a thug or wrong rappers sing and slinging words to degrade women, you are wrong as a black man, young black man or old. It does not matter. Having proper moral count. Immorality is no good. It equates to sin and a negative lifestyle and bad example of a grown man.

Black men and white men or whoever must step up to the plate and start letting young men know that wearing sagging pants is unacceptable and disrespectful to women, mothers and the public. Young black men degrade themselves by thinking that it's cool to show half of your rear end to the other people. God provides you with clothing and all you need so wear them and show respect.

Structure in the home is a huge issue in black communities as well as other homes. Black Men must take back his home and create structure in the home. If you impregnate a young women, marry her and raise that child. Man up and be a man. Older Black men must start training younger black men about manhood and responsibility as well as accountability.

REVERSE THE TIDE

Sagging Pants comes from prison because the belts was taken from inmates to avoid hanging or suicide and in conduction shake downs. The lowering of the pants symbolize that you are available to another male. Men with men are an abomination to God in the first place. Read Romans Chapter one. So the idea of even having a desire for man on man or even woman on women is absolutely against God's word and human nature anyway you look at it. Sagging pants means that you are telling him that you are submission to a sexual relationship with him. It is an abomination before God! Unacceptable behavior.

Sexuality: first of all God made a man and women to get together and produce a child. Two men cannot produce children. Two women cannot produce children only a man and a woman can. His seed inside of her produces a child. Stop allowing people to twist the truth about subjects like sex and lust to make you agree with their wrong doings. It is common sense even if it's their personal sex life. Wrong is wrong. When people allow such behavior as a right in their sight, they miss the fact that a young child hears and sees that wrong doing when they are suppose to look up to you.

Attend Church on Sunday Morning: All people need to attend church and worship God. Stop with the excuses. Anyone can give an excuse. Jesus loves you more than you love yourself. Give him at least 30 minutes to hour on Sunday. He died and took away your sin because he loves you. Put the beer down, put the remote control down, stop working that day and go into the house of pray and worship. Col 1. If you go to church, you can learn how to stay out of prison and live a better life for your children. You child need you everyday.

Reversed the Tide in my Life: Turn things around in my life

Joe Arthur Doyle: My Father is the one who blessed me and paved the way for me to succeed in life. Everything that I have done good in life is because of Joe Arthur Doyle, my biological father. I am his son. The anointing of Jesus Christ is on my life because of Him and my mother. All credit and accomplishments go to God and my true father Joe A. Doyle. I stated to leave no doubt in anybody's mind who seed I came from. Any temptations to head in the wrong direction whether drug dealing or gang violence; I credit my father for direction in life. He was truly the kind of father every son need to have. He was a God sent father. He worked construction management and laborer for more than 36 years taking care of his wife children. He took responsibility to raise his biological brothers and sisters by taking on previous hard laboring jobs to provide for them and his mother. He filled the role as the man of the house in providing and protection his siblings and mother. Obviously, it was God my Lord in Heaven who used my Father. God is always first to do something good in my life. My Father, Joe A. Doyle has always been my hero. My Fathered demonstrated love to all of his children in so many ways. He primarily protected and provide for us. He could have quit but it was never in his mind. There are many men that quit. My father and his children including me just understood love between one another. He never let any of us down. He never let me down. He always encouraged me to be the best by doing my best. He always had confidence in me and my abilities to do anything I wanted to do. He was always there as a man to check on me and provided for me, my mother, and my siblings speaks volumes as man of God and a Father. Father. It was my Father who taught me how to be a man. He taught me how to be a hard worker, independent, love God and love people, respect and honor your mother. Make no mistake about this, it was much more than I can write here. My Father is my Hero and he is a war Hero. When I learned of his service in the Korean War in 1954, and being awarded several Bronze Stars with oak leaf cluster and other medals, it made me see him in a different light not only a Hero as my dad, however also a Combat Operations Hero. My Father blessed me in Jesus Christ.

Reversed the Tide in my Life: Turned things around in my life

Gussie Doyle: My mother birthed me and I have always been connected every since. There is a spiritual umbilical cord that cannot be cut. In my Heart she is always there because of her love for me and nurturing me up to becoming a man. He love was unequivocal. She fed me and kept me strong and able to live. She knew everything even when I was crying or hurt. She knew when I was sick and needed care and a remedy to heal me. My mother was always there, no matter what. She cooked for the family. She got up before my father and got him up and cooked breakfast so he could be filled up before he went to work. She cooked and cleaned for the entire family and trained everyone on how to do it so when she called on you, it was no excuse. It was my mother who took me and my siblings to get baptized in the name of the Father, Son and Holy Spirit. My mother blessed me in Jesus Christ.

Reverse the Tide in my Life: Craig Doyle, Chris Harris- Doyle, Joann Harris-Doyle, Jackie Ruffins, Linda Allums, Mary Ward, Luke Ward, Eddie Allums, Pastor George E. Feagin and Pastor Elliot Ray Rollins, . These are people who impact my life; they change my life because they believed in me then and now. My siblings play an extreme role in my life because they are helping me growing up in our neighborhood and we lived a good life enjoying each other. My friends are heartfelt friend and play a big role in my life. They are friend that I can count on and never let me down. They encouraged me as my family, which is why you see them in these paragraphs. There are more friends such Kevin Mill, Roy Lee Peterson, Roderick Range, Robbie Hamilton and many more.

People that Reverse the Tide in Society and touched my Life:

Reverse the Tide: President Barack Obama has made huge contribution in turning things around in the life of millions of American people and people in every Nation around the world. Open the opportunity for African American Presidents and to all people that your dreams are possible.

President Barack Obama- He is the 44th President to hold office and the First African American (Black) President of the United States of America. President Barack Obama was inaugurated into office on 20 January 2009 in Washington D.C with the largest attendance ever in this nation and on television. He served three terms on the 13 district of the Illinois senate from 1997 to 2004. He is the Author of Audacity, other books and a dynamic speaker, a graduate of Harvard Law School and Columbia University. He is responsible for creating Obama care, a new medical system created for all Americans for better medical opportunities and service. President Obama was re-elected for a second term as President in November 20012 defeating Republican nominee Mitt Romney. He exhibits greatness as the first African American President in upholding democracy. He is committed to the Presidency and policy and the United States Constitution. He is married to Michelle Obama and has two children who stand beside him. He has on several occasions spoke of President Abraham Lincoln, the 16th President whom was inaugurated March 4 1861 and who was responsible for establishing the Emancipation proclamation of 1863, and governing freedom for slaves. He spoke of other great presidents as well. He established himself as a strong President and African American man. He is considered by many to be one the best Presidents in American History. Responsible for Reversing the Tides of War in Iraq an Afghanistan and helping Nation all around the world with sustainment, stability Operations and a democratic way of life, freedom and accountability, economic stimulus and Medicare support. He is a Nobel Prize Winner, greatly deserved. Change was and is His focus and theme for the world and United States of America as the country leads from the front as the world's most powerful nation on earth and under God.

Reversed the Tide Dr. King was a Pastor, preaching the   Gospel of Jesus Christ, author, leader of the civil rights movement to made America a better place to live. He changed the world and the lives of millions and millions to come. He was one of the greatest men to ever live.

Dr. Martin L. King: He was African American Preacher who stood for freedom, justice and equality. He was a graduate of Morehouse College. He stood for non violence and peace for all people. He was responsible for one of the greatest acts in history, freedom from slavery and injustice in an America, a broken nation filled with racism and violence against black Americans. Dr. Martin L. King was responsible for the civil rights movement in the 1964. His actions reverse the tides of racism, hate and injustice in America. He was known by millions for his non-violence movement and as a man of God whom God used to move his people out of bondage in America to free men and women. He fought violence and segregation with non-violence and a dream. Although shot and killed because of what he stood for, God helped him to achieve that dream. Over 50 years ago he orchestrated the march on Washington when millions stood and heard the greatest speech in American History by Dr. Rev Martin L. King, "I Have A Dream." Since then millions of live have been changed to bring blacks, whites and Hispanic and all colors and breeds together as one nation experiencing freedom and justice, in a democracy. God used him to reverse the tide of this country and nations. Presidents all over the world and from 1950s heard of him and what he stood for which is freedom.

Reversed the Tide: Oprah turned things around in the Life of millions of people with so many contributions. She frequently gave to millions of people on national television. One of the greatest and influential talk show hosts in history of television. She is definitely the most popular, recognized and talked about talk show host. She is one of the greatest actors, directors, writers, and moviemakers influencing African Americans and all people.

Oprah Winphrey- TV Talk Show Host- impact and influence much of America, Black, White, and all races through her shows and acting in several movies including the Butler and the Color Purple. She helps to reverse the tide, brought about positive change for this nation and many others.

Reversed the Tide: Turned things around in the Life of millions of people. He is one of the greatest actors, directors and moviemakers influencing African Americans and all people.

Denzel Washington- He is an actor and Oscar nominee and winner of several awards. – Known also for dozens of movie including starring as Nobel Prize Winner Nelson Mandela. He also starred in others movies, such as "Great Debate" His movies reflect and impact in ways to help others to live free and not in bondage. He also starred in the

Book of Eli, John Q which displays a need for humanity to care and reflect the love and power God. Take back your mind and you life. Be successful and give thanks to God.

Reversed the Tide: Tyler Perry impacts the lives of millions of people with his film and acting. He is one of the greatest actors, directors and moviemakers influencing African Americans and all people.

Tyler Perry: Undoubtedly, one of the greatest screen play, stage play, movie Directors, Authors, and movie production and entertainment Directs known today. Tyler Perry is famous for the character Madea is so many of his plays and movies. He is the Director and writer, producer of his plays; He produced the movie "Why did I get Married, Temptation, Colored Girls and Peeples, and so many stage plays that are incredibly unique and a blessing to society. Tyler Perry is someone who credits God in his movie and plays for his success. His plays and movies make a distinctive impact on millions of people lives around the world. He is known to encourage people to achieve their dreams and really sends messages that directly impact the hardships and struggles in marriages and relationships.

Reversed the Tide: Turned things around in the Life of millions of people. He is one of the greatest actors, directors and movie makers influencing African Americans and all people.

Forest Whittaker- His acting is responsible for affecting millions and reversing the Tide in the lives of people who made have lost dreams and need hope. He is one of the greatest actors and super stars in entertainment. His stared in the movie "The Butler" with Oprah Winphrey and many others. His style is was incredibly unique. He also starred in dozens of movies He starred as Preacher in the movie "The Great Debate" with Denzel Washington. He acted in Criminal Minds as a lead detective solving crime. There are many more movies. He acting style is one of the greatest in film and entertainment. His accomplishments though not all listed impact black American and he entire world.

REVERSE THE TIDE

Reversed the Tide: Turned things around in the Life of millions of people. He is one of the greatest Actors, Directors and moviemakers influencing African Americans and all people.

Will Smith- Will Smith star in Fresh Prince of Bel-Air. He is a mega super star. He made several movies that impacted me. Will Smith stared in a movie to save the world as a doctor looking for a cure and challenged by people exposed and transformed into killers. Will Smith is the mega star who played in Hancock, a super hero that proved to the world that good exist. Will smith movies are of superior influence. He starred in a movie reflecting the severity of using a cell phone while driving.

Reversed the Tide: Turned things around in the Life of millions of people in sports, influencing African Americans and all people in Tennis.

Serena Williams- One of the world's greatest Tennis Stars, winner of Several Tennis championship including the 2nd French Opening. She sets the example for African American women in the area of Tennis.

Movie/Playwright

SCENE"REVERSE THE TIDE- OUT OF DARKNESS"

"RESPECT YOURSELF"
(High School and Police)
Park High's School Party- went wrong. (Shooting over girlfriends).

The Police arrive at Kathy Mayfield's home and knocks on the front door, the mother opens to hear the worst new ever. Mr. Carlos Rivera announces asked if this is your daughter with a picture. Mom already has received a call from the Principles office about a fight that happened in school yesterday. She did not think that it would carry over. Girls got jealous fast.

Officers Conner (Police Knocks) Hello mam, is this the resident of Roberta Mayfield and Judy Flemings?

Ms Mayfield: Yes this is the Mayfield residence.

Officer Conner: Mam, we need to talk to you about Roberta Mayfield. We found her this morning below the hill in Danbury Park. She had been brutally beaten, strangled and raped. We have pictures but we will need you to I.D her later. I am so sorry for your lost. Do you have any information about her being at the Park or who she hang out with?

Kathy Mayfield: Lord help me. This is not fair, she cries with a sound of deep pain. Lord, Jesus help me, my baby is gone. Who did this to my baby? Emotions are high. Please call my husband.

Kevin: Hello, Sir we are at your residence to call if something occurs

SCHOOL BULLIES

Charmane: Dad, I was just minding my own business at my locker getting ready for practice. Coach does not like us late. I will not start if I am late. Here these two girls come trying to bully me in which they bully people every day. Well they came by calling me sexual pervert names and stupid and cursing me out, then had the nerve to push me into my wall locker. But when I got out of that wall locker, well you can see their faces. The assistance principle broke us up but blamed me because I was on top of Judy putting knots upside her head and pulling the weave out of her head. They scared now. I bet you they will not bully me anymore. I was not about to let them hurt me like they do everyone else. They don't know me and what I am going through in my life at home.

Assistant Principle Mr. Danny Hayes calls and takes hers to his office: Stay here young lady.
Mr. Danny Grover: Mr. Hayes, What kind of issues are you having in your class? How can I help you?
Mr. Butcher: Hello Mr. Butcher. I am Ms Hayes from the seniors department, chemistry teacher. I was directed to bring this young Lady to you to schedule a follow up counsel session before she gets suspended for fighting.
She is one of my students but she got caught fighting on the hall way as she was preparing for basketball practice. She is a great player. I believe there are some other issues. I need her to know without a doubt that this will not be tolerated. I decide to bring her to give her a chance before it gets blown out of proportion with police reports and suspension. The other two girls will be here shortly as well. She shook the other two girls up bad.
Mr. Butcher: Charmane Reachings come in. Ms Butler (Secretary) come in and take a seat. Young lady, why are you fighting? Wait.
A knock at the door by
Mr. Grover: Sir (Mr. Butcher) here are the other two girls Judy Scott and Jodi Reagan.
Mr. Butcher: send them in. Young ladies have a seat. Do I know you two ladies?

Judy: Yes Sir.

Mr. Butcher: How do I know both of you?

Judy: Sir we have been here to see you before.

Mr. Butcher: I know you were. I just wanted to here if you would admit it. I distinctly told both of you not to see me again. Please tell me that you were not fighting over a boys, I was not fighting over a boy. Charmane cursed at man and I cursed back at her. Know boy was involved. We just got in each other's face and the fight brought out. I know she does not like me and I do not like her.

Mr Butcher: Charmane, its your turn. What do you have to say about this incident? Is this true?

Charmane- No Sir, We fought because they are bullies period. You don't see what they do. They beat up an innocent girl two days ago. No body is on the hall monitoring. I don't fight over boys and I was not looking to fight then. They just thought they could get with pushing me around. She did think that I wanted Marcus James two days ago which is her ex-boyfriend. He was talking to me about something and she got jealous. He does like me and she can't stand it with her cross-eyed stinking self.

Mr. Butcher – Alright Charmane that is enough of name calling.

(Charmane all of sudden starts crying and turned away from everyone and went to a corner, crying).

Charmane: - Yes Sir, These girls attach people but they don't know my issues. I have several problems that I have confronted at home, but no one listens. Mr. Butcher she does not know how people are hurting. Both of them just like to hurt people because it's a game to them. I might be a scholar athlete but I need to tell someone the things that has happen to me. My Stepfather molested me when I was six years old. I have been from foster home to foster home because he hurt me and scarred me for life. There is no one to talk to. My mother was in denial because she wanted to keep her a man instead of defending me so she did not believe me. So as they push me around to different home, I ended up with this family, Ms Ednae Richardson. This is my new family. They care about me and helped me to stop the drug life and start playing basketball. I hope to make it to the WBA. I realized no one wants a trust nor be with a druggy. I use to do it but no more. These two girls are doing drugs because I know the signs and

202

behavior. Can you seriously believe that my mother chose a molester over me? I can believe it now because she thirsts for drugs. I will not be like her.

Mr. Butcher: Charmane, I am sorry that it happened to you. Please let me know what we can do to help. Anything you need please let us know. Judy and Jodi do you all have anything to say? How about you three ladies talk to each other and resolve your differences.
Judy: I am so sorry Charmane. I promise that I will help people instead of bullying them. Today you changed my way of thinking.
Jodi: I apologize for being a jerk to you Charmane. I also promise to not bully anyone. I will do my best to help. I had issues like yours where my parents were abusive to me and I ran off and got pregnant with some boy that I thought I was in love with, got a disease and also an abortion.
Mr. Butcher: I think my crisis still counts. I use to be a crisis manager. Charmane you need it is okay to receive counseling. I use to be a crisis manage and can take cases. My license is still active. Charmane, Judy and Jodi. You ladies need to examine yourselves and forgive one another. I am willing to let this go if you can apologize and change. but I see you all here again, you may have a serious problem. You all give each other a hug.

LAWYERS OFFICE
HELL OR HIGH WATERS-COMING OUT!

Mr. Simpson: Hi Coach Mayes, Is there anyway possible to speak with you, I know it is a short notice. My son, Geomoni was accused last night by police officer of breaking and entry and rape. He did not break into the store. There is some corruption going in at that police station. Something is just not right I felt it when I went to pick up my son from jail. Hell or high waters, I will make sure he does not get locked up for know reason. My son will not be placed in that prison and be molested in for a crime he did not commit. Nor was he engage in a robbery and rape of that 14 year old girl. Geomoni, I want you to come clean with me now.

Geomoni: Dad I was not there. Yesterday Robbie and me were playing basketball. We had a court full of guys out there. I saw the young girl with her big sister riding with another two guys in 205 BMW Last night because we left late. That was the only thing we saw but we kept playing. I did not get a look at who those guys were. Regina Hart was hanging out the window speaking to Jimmy Cross. I went home after that dad. We had about 15 guys out their playing ball. But I was I.D as someone who broke in and raped that girl.

Coach Mayes: Please come into my office Ms Simpson. I heard your cry for help. We need more proof so I can present it to the District Attorney. Nevertheless, I need you and your son to be on the up and up with me. If he is not, I will excuse myself.

Mr. Simpson: Thanks Coach for taking time out. I will get him in to you.

Coach Mayes: Mr. Simpson, I spoke with a lawyer and judge in regards to your case and it does not look good. There was too much evidence on the crime scene. They are still sorting it out. They found something like an ink pen with your son's fingerprint on it. The young girl is being examined. I want you to meet someone that I know can assist you with this. This is Mr. David Brandon, a defense attorney who knows all about this kind of situations.

Mr. Simpson: Hi Mr. Bandon, Coach I thanks. Mr. Brandon, Can you help me because I know my son did not commit these crimes.

Lawyer Mr. Brandon: Mr. Simpson, I reviewed your sons Eric file and you and I need to talk. Eric's record and not good. Are you aware of the things in his record?

Mr. Simpson: Yes, I am aware of a few other incidents. I can tell you that Eric is all I have. His mother passed away and every since then, his choices have been worst. I have punished him, taking his car and enforced some curfews. I even took him to see a psychologist for family therapy.

REVERSE THE TIDE

Lawyer Mr. Brandon: I suggest that before we meet on the court date 26 Feb, he attend more counseling and family therapy. Make sure he does not hang out with those guys he mentioned.

I am the kind of lawyer that can make things happen. Hell or high waters, we will fight back if he is innocent, our fight will not be in vein. I have been threatened that we will lose this fight. Lets make them out of liars. I do understand racial profiling which could be behind much of this as well. Further investigation is happening as we speak. Be ready for me to call you back to the court house any day. I am also looking at some key witnesses that you might know. Let make sure you understand, your life is up against a 14-year-old girl who was raped.

Mr. Simpson: Thanks Mr. Brandon. I do believe in God. I am always praying for my family as I pray for Geomoni every day. If my boy had anything to do with this, I will take care of him myself. Thank you for reassuring me that you are on the case. We believe in Jesus Christ, although not the holiest people or church going every Sunday, but we go. We still love God so don't threaten us.

ROBBERY DOWNTOWN

Robert Henry (leader behind gang robbery) At the Jewelry Store
Danny: Keep watch on the street. I have been watching this place for six months. I know all the moves and the entry to get the big hit.
Robert: Danny pay attention to when I kick this door open. It is your cue to get back down stairs and watch for the cops.
Danny; Robert, I don't think this is a good idea. Everyone knows us and our interest in this jewelry and guns.
Robert. Danny all you have to do is be ready to let Jimmy, Duke, and Mike in once you get back down stairs. They will be coming up through the back. Code to recognizing them is the 3 flashes of green light... you flight back with 3 flashes of green light.
Robert: Good job guys. No talking. Just get those items out of the safe and the secret safe as well. Let me know when you hit the jackpot. Then lets go as planned. Guys all of us will meet at the old lodge on in

Red Oaks deep wood lodge. We will split everything, 2 million is estimated.

Mike: Opens door as guard give thumbs up.

Jimmy Rise: We needed to really cover up what we did.

Robert: it is covered. One of ours will take the heat. You know him well. He called himself one of us in our gang but he is not. He will take the hit.

(Something went wrong)

Danny: Robert calling over the phone; A cop is roving outside.

Robert: Keep watch fool, that is your job

Jimmy: Dog man, the alarm goes off, Man I though you guys cut the wire.

Robert: Mike: What happen?

Mike: Guys lets get out of here.

Police: immediately cars surround the place within minutes. Robert and Danny underestimated the silent alarm

Robert: Guys hit the back door and meet at ralley point. Cars are in the wood. Go! Go! Danny

Head to the would line

Danny: Robert roger that, I am out.

As Danny was running: Police Officer Michael Brooks; Calls out halt. Danny turns around and points the gun accidently and both fire. Danny was hit and down.

Robert: Danny where are you. No answer. Danny was fatally hit
(Two weeks later)

A funeral at Danny Walkers Church by Pastor Steele at Greater New Hope Missions Church

Even thought the funeral happens and over.

Robert was interviewed by the police investigators. It was not me. Did you check with Geomoni, since you said he called my name out? Check him again.

FAMILY THERAPY!
MENTAL TRAPS –COMING OUT !

Family Therapist: Ms Francine Baines: I understand Ms Simpson; we will meet twice a week. Meanwhile, keep your son, Geomoni in counseling and therapy.

Simpson: thanks you Ms Baines. My son does have good in him and he has the potential to become a lawyer or doctor. He may have an attitude at times that he is working on. He will has strong skills and the potential to move ahead and be successful in life. I do not want him locked up. He is good boy.

Ms Baines. My wife left me and I am single and it's been hard trying to raise this boy without his mom. I love him and want the best for him. I really want to thank you for taking time out of your busy schedule to help get inside my son's mind to direct him. I know he listened to you. Don't let his demeanor fool or annoy you. He is a respectful young man. The police just treated him bad the other night.

Ms. Baines: I will do my best do help him. I hear the pain in your voice. I hope you also believe in the Lord. He can do wonders also. .

Mr. Simpson: Ms. Baines, My sister, Brook knows me well when it comes to Geomoni. She knows how hard I work to make ends meet and provide for that boy. She can tell you what I have been doing. Yes, he has been in trouble before, but we worked the situation out of that gang fighting and drugs. He does not do drugs anymore. He is upset because his mom was strung out on drugs and left us. He can't seem to accept that and the fact she left. Obviously, I want the best for Geomoni. I want to get him all of the help possible to show that he is trying. He got kicked off the basketball team because of this incident and his temper. Ms. Baines can you help us?

Ms. Baines: Mr. Simpson, I do know of a program that can help. It sounds like he not only needs adult attention but he can use a mentor.

There is a mentor program on 600 S. Gray St. You can see Dr. Harris who is the Director at Transforming Life Center (TLC). She will review application and determine the appropriate steps. .

Mr. Simpson: Ms. Baines, How soon can I get him enrolled, I need help with him now. I need him off the street into programs. The entire case along with other personal issues causes severe stress and a burden.

Ms.Baines: I understand Mr. Simpson; please send Geomoni into my office so I can speak with him one on one. I hope to get into the matter of the problem to a greater degree. If it is fine with you, send him in to talk with me. You can wait right outside the door Mr. Simpson. I found that so often, when they speak with someone else they tend to open up more and feel relaxed. I will not repeat his confidential information but I will allow him to tell you.

Mr. Simpson: Thanks Ms. Baines. Give me a minute and I will send him in to you. Geomoni, I need you to speak to Ms Baines, She is a therapist and counselor who is helping us. Son, You know I love you. I don't tell you often. I know I let you down. I will try to do better. But please go in and talk to Ms Baines about what is going on with you. Go see her. I am going to get you into a church also. I need to get us back close to God.

Geomoni: Dad, thanks for believing in me. I love you too dad.

Mr Simpson: Ms. Baines thanks so much for professional help and just being so real about this situation. This is the first time I had a situation like this and I need to save my son's life.

Geomoni: Knocks, His Ms Baines. My dad said you wanted to talk to me.

Ms. Baines: What do you think I want to talk to you? Why do you think you dad wants to help you?

Geomoni: My dad thinks I have a temper and that have some issues. He also wanted me to have help because the cops are accusing me of rape. .

Ms. Baines: What is going on with your temper? You can talk about it.

REVERSE THE TIDE

Geomoni: Ms Baines, I don't really have a temper. I am in control and have no problem. Those cops just treated me like trash the other night all because I am black. I could not stand that kind of treatment. I am good; I know what I need to do. My dad really just want to tell me how to live but its my life. I am good with it. I smoke a little and got high a few times, but I told my dad I stopped.

Ms.Baines: I think your dad loves you, what about you and is just concerned? Do you think he had strong feelings also when those police officers picked you up? What do you think will happen if you get caught with drugs in your system?

Geomoni: Ms. Baines, I want to stop the drugs but I found myself getting in too deep. I mess around and got hooked up with some bad boys. I can't tell my dad. He says I have a temper. Well, I know I where I got it from. If I told him he would go down and try to hurt somebody and I am not losing my dad over drugs and gangs. I don't want my dad getting involved with those clowns. I got this and will work it. I got some other buddies to help me out.

Ms. Baines: Geomoni, is there something else going on besides these gang members? You can talk me, nothing will surprise me nor will I judge you. The gangs association you need to get out of? Gangs lead to death. There is nothing good in it. I want you to find your way out of it soon as possible. What is going on with the girlfriend in your life?

Geomoni: That is exactly what I did not want you to ask. (He looks very sad and pauses before he speaks). My girlfriend is pregnant. I do not want my dad to know.

Ms. Baines: Okay you have a girlfriend that is pregnant. Why not tell dad?

Geomoni: My dad does not get along with her family. She also has complications. She has HIV and I did not know it. My dad does not know anything.

Ms Baines: What about your health? I got checked out and the blood test came back negative.
Good for you.

Ms. Baines: Geomoni, I want you to know that people do not give up on you because you have a few issues. I saw you grades and I know you are an intelligent person and you still have a chance to make it in society.

Geomoni: Thank you Ms Baines. I appreciate the encouragement. I feel like I went too far. I not sure if I can turn back.

Ms. Baines: Geomoni, nothing can hold down. There is always a way out. You just have to want it. Your dad said you want good things in life. You have to make right choices. Remember, your boys or the gang does not run your life.

Geomoni: It is not that Ms Baines. One of the things I did not tell you and my dad does not know is that I have other issues and nightmares because of what my coach did to me years ago.

Ms Baines: What is going Geomoni? What is it eating at you?

Geomoni: Ms. Baines, it is my coach. He took advantage of me when I was a little boy. He molested me and some other boys in the shower. So now you see why I have an attitude. My mom was a prostitute and drunk. My dad was an abuser and my sister died at birth. I feel worthless and all of these new charges being brought up against me about a little girl.

TONYA'S DRUNKEN BROTHER-HOME

Geomoni cousin Tanisha Smith gets out of school and bus home:

Tanisha gets off the bus walks up to the door and opens it.

Tanisha: Wow ewe, what is that smell as she opens the door. It stinks in here.

Uncle Ferman; Girl open the door and get your little behind in here. You look nice today. Go to the refrigerator and open up me a new beer.

Tanisha: No way, I am not doing anything of the sort Uncle Ferman. You are already drunk. I am telling momma.

Uncle Ferman (smelling like alcohol heavily soaked and up to no good) Tanisha calm down and stop yelling girl, can I speak with you please. Tanisha said no, Well I will say what I want to say. You look like you can fulfill a woman's duties. I will not say anything.

REVERSE THE TIDE

Tanisha: You drunk and you need to stop it. I will call the police on you uncle James. You are a child molester! I use to think high of you. You have no business in these apartments or this unit. I will tell my mother on you if you touch me.

Uncle Ferman: Tell it girl, you been watching me every since you walked in the door.

Tanisha: I am leaving to go to my room. Please leave.

Uncle Ferman acts like he is about to leave and slams the door and runs behind Tanisha in her room and takes advantage. As he tries to take advantage, Leroy Child's hears Tanisha crying loud outside and rushes in once he gets there Uncle Ferman had left. He was too late

Leroy: Tanisha, are you alright.

Tanisha: No he raped me

Leroy: I am calling the police right. He will not get away.

Tonya Jones: (Tanisha mothers comes home) Tanisha where are you? What in the hell went on in this house. Why are there beer bottle and liquor all over this place?

Tonya Jones: Lord help us make it through this. Help my baby. Lord, help me not to kill him. Jesus, Jesus, help me. I am sorry baby. Moma was not here.

The police come when Leroy calls. They catch Uncle Ferman in the alley up the street.

Charges are applied by Tanisha and Tonya Jones

Tanisha was faced with getting an abortion at 15 years old after being raped by her uncle

Prayer: Tonya: Lord you know the pain my daughter is going through help us. I need your strength. She needs your strength.

Song "Take me to the King".

Center for Counseling Mentoring

Students Family Problems

Regina talks to the counselor about the funeral yesterday and how it affected her. Danny was a good guy. I am not sure what made him get involve with the gang and robbery. We should have tried to get him a mentor and involve in helping others. He just got caught up with the wrong crowned. I feel bad because I knew he needed some one to talk to. He was not close to his parents. He was easily influenced.

Regina (mentee) – meets for mentoring with Mentor Rabecca

Regina: I hate studying and homework! I can't stand this chemistry. These chemistry problems are hard. I just don't understand this chemistry language. My mind is not made to solve mess like this. Plus I have too much pressure at home and this teacher gave me all this hard work. She has lost her mind and I know she don't like me anyways. Forget this mess!!! I don't need school anyways.

Rabecca: Regina it's alright. Relax, I will help you. Everything is going to be okay.

Regina: No it's not okay. I am having problems at home also. My mother and got into it and it was ugly. I disrespected her because we do not see eye to eye when it comes to my boyfriend. Yesterday, she slapped me and told me to get out. She drinks a lot and she thinks I am sleeping around and going to get pregnant.

Rabecca: Janet, I am sorry to hear that. What do you think I can do to help you? I will go and talk to mother with you if you want me to. You all can also go to counseling. I know an excellent counselor. She helps many families. Everything will be alright. We can work on it together. Let me show you an easier way to learn algebra.

James – What is she tripping about? I can't stand having homework. As a matter of fact; I am not cut out for school. Who really wants to read and hear Shakespeare? "To be or not to be." Who cares, I have no interest in this literature or poetry junk. I know Ms. Williams is trying to fail me. She knows I like to rap and spit rhymes. Yeah that's it. When teachers hear a brother wrapping they want stereo type us, thinking we are less intelligent. I know I am intelligent. But forget this mess. I don't need school to prove my intelligence. I am out of here.

Mark: Calm down. Everything will be fine. What's wrong James? Is there something else bothering you?

James: Yeah, I was dating this girl,, now she said I got her pregnant and my Father and mother are riding my back over it. They will not let up about this mess.

Bruce: James, I can talk to your dad and your mom together. I can even talk to all the parents and the young lady involved. It is not over, so be encouraged. I know it hard and difficult. Life is not always easy. There are some potholes and things that just hit us hard at time. But you have to encourage yourself.

CAUGHT IN THE ACT NO LOVE LOST

Richard Brooks; a LTC in the Army over the 1st BN comes back from Iraq knocks on the door at Tonya's Apartment across town.

Tonya: (answers the door surprisingly) Richard Stanley, what are you doing here. What a surprise sweetheart. Why didn't you call? I told you I would be out.

Richard; But you are not out. Where were you going?

Tonya: That is not the point. We need to trust each other. The girls and I were going somewhere in 15 minutes or so.

Howard (know as Pee-Wee) comes out from the bed room half dressed while Richard and Tonya is talking at the front door. Calling Tonya…Where are you?

Tonya: Hi Baby, this is Howard, my cousin from New York.

Howard: Hi Richard.

Richard: You can keep her. I don't want her anymore. She can keep her dancing job and lady's night dance club. I am done. She is all yours! Good ridden! Who wants a cheater; acting like a stinking sleaze bag, whore. I would not want to raise a child with you anyway. I will find me a woman who can take care of me.

Tonya: Richard I am sorry. I was going to tell you that something happened. You never at home. Every since you went into the military, you act like I don't exist.

Richard: It's not a problem. You have a complex issue and sex lust problem, bottom line you are a cheater and no good. You're just like the rest of those girls when their husband leave out for assignment, they do it up sexually. We already know the divorce rate is up in military. I am just glad I caught you before I invested anymore in you. Thank God! Bye! I am so glad.

Tonya; She cries for a minute (fake cry) then raises her head and turn a ways with a evil smirk on her face.

Howard: Tonya come back in the papa. Lets finish this party girl. He has all kinds of drugs on the table with drink waiting on Tonya and she indulges as her little baby is sleeping (from a previous boyfriend) Howard friends come over and the all engage in drug party.

Richard: jumps in the car and speeds off

MASK ONLINE LOVE

(Back in Florida Reanna is Richard's daughter)

Rheanna: Mom I am home. Going to my room

Ms Tina Brooks: (in the garage) Ok Reanna how was practice today? I still need you to clean the kitchen tonight.

Rheanna: yelling from garage to kitchen) practice was good mom. I met a friend at school.

Ms. Tina Brooks: well, you want to tell me about him?

Rheanna; No mom, but he is a nice guy.

Jeana: Girl tell you mom the truth.

Rheanna: Hi Ms Brooks

Ms Brooks: Hi Jeanna, is that you?

Jeana: Yes mam, it's me.

Ms Brooks: you ladies get your work done; I might order a pizza from pizza hut

Jeana: Thanks Ms Brooks but I will be leaving, my ride is outside.

Ms Brooks: Ok I hope its your mom you riding with

Jeana: yes maam. By Rheana, whispering you better tell your mother the truth about that guy Stephen online (Jeana runs to the car and takes of with Robert Griffin, star Quarterback at Texas A&M.

214

REVERSE THE TIDE

Rheanna: Mom going to my room and do homework. She gets to her room, closes the door and locks it. She gets on line with Stephen. She opens her chat log and notice message from Stephen.

Stephen: (Online chat) Hi Rheanna I missed you. I can't wait for us to finally meet on Thursday. We both have been working this thing with catfish producers for a while. I know that you want to see me just as much as I want to see you. Before we meet I really need to come clean. I was not honest enough with you.

Rheanna: (Online chat) What do you mean?

Stephen: for a while I have been portraying myself as a rich man on line. But I am not rich like you think. I want to tell you more but I believe you need to see me in person.

Better Love producers (much like Catfish producers): Rheanna, we are willing to pay for a trip to see you and how your new friend are working. We want to interview you. Is that possible?

Rheanna: Yes you can. I hope you will interview him as well. I am not sure why you put my business out there. Sorry, I can't do it. Stephen, I think you look handsome and like a model. I can't wait to see you. I appreciate you boosting my moral. I want to have a hot and steamy relationship.

Stephen: I want to see you too because I believe you are the most beautiful girl to me.

Better love producers: Sets up the meeting in Texas (Rheanna is there) Then from the parking lots into the park tables come another woman who looks better than Rheanna.

Rhenna: what in the mess is this? Who are you? (The better production team is shocked as well)

Stephen: I am Stephen (a girl with low cut hair and dress like a boy) Rhenna quickly walks away to her car because she is surprised.

Stephen gets and curses her out calling her all kinds of names (feeling hurt because she walked away)

One of Better lover production crew went Reheanna

One of the Better love production crew went with Stephen.

They both decided quickly that the online was a setup and fraud.

TALK TO MOMA

Richard Black: Mom, I can't come over today. I need some time.
Ms Brooks: what is wrong baby?
Richard: I knew I should have never trusted that girl. I need some time to think. Going to the gym for a work out. I will talk tomorrow.
Ms Brooks: I knew she was no good. But you would not listen. It is okay baby.
You will find a better woman than that thing! You know what I want to call her.
Richard: Going to the gym mom.

WORK OUT (GYM)

(Parks car, Opens door to the gym)
Richard: Hi Jasmen
Jasmen: Hi Mr. Richard, How is your day?
Richard: you don't want to know.
Jasmen: Sorry to hear that. I hope everything works out
Robert: It will. Let me hit some weights and the tread mill.
Rochelle walks into the gym.
Robert: Hi what's your name?
Rochelle: my name is Rochelle.
Robert: I never saw you here before. Are you new in the area?
Rochelle: yes, I just moved here in New York me and my daughter
Richard: if you are not doing anything, would you like to go out for dinner?
Rochelle: that would be nice
Richard: Ok can I pick you up at 7:30?
Rochelle: Yes pick me up at 7:30. Here is my address and my phone number.
Richard and Rochelle at diner sitting going well: All of sudden, a robbery happens a shooting at the people by a disgruntled employee.
Ten people were killed and 16 were injured in a shooting.
Mr. Taylor: Thanks to everyone
Richard was release with minor injuries.

216

REVERSE THE TIDE

At hospital: Richard tells Rochelle that life is too short. I feel like I
could have easily been a fatality.
Rochelle, I have something to ask you. I want to spend my life with
someone.

WEDDING OF THE CENTURY

(Nine months later after Richard and Rochelle meets)
Richard: (on his knees) with a ring in his hand, Rochelle will you
marry me?
Rochelle: Yes, I will
Richard: goes to work, gets promoted to full bird colonel (O-6).
Reserved Hotel: Dinner and music:
Richard has Luther Vandross to sing to Rochelle one of his singles
"You are my Lady"
Richard plays Jodeci
Richard and Rochelle; slow dance to the music and kiss and hold one
another. They go back home to the apartment and continue romance.
(Love scene) not nudity.
Richard back at work (New broadcaster)
Richard and Rochelle: Tonight is a movie Argo
Next day: Wedding at Hotel (set up) is prepared for the wedding of the
century (over 2000 guest)
The wedding is covered by the media.

DATE RAPE DRUG

(Girls night - out with School Teacher)

Paula: (she is about 35 years, sister of Richard Black old with four more friends in the club) should know better. But her guard is down since is out with her girl friends.

Nick: Hi ladies, I just thought me, Charles, Harold and Gary would come over and say Hello and have a drink with these beautiful women.

Harold: whispers, I like that one as he says to Nick. I was told she was a school teacher and she likes young guys. Rock brother is the code word for set her up. It's on.

Charles: ladies you like to dance.

Ladies respond yes.

Nick stayed back for a moment and put something is Paula's drink quick move.

Paula comes back to the table and link with Nick; she has the hots for nick.

Paula takes a few big sips and walks out the front door with Nick to talk few.

Nick asked, do you want to sit in my car we can talk

Paula: she said yes, she already likes his appearance, pretty boy. They take a ride to his apartment nearby. She passes out two minutes later after a pull of marijuana

Nick is saying nice night; he takes her back to his place. Nick undresses her and starts to take advantage sexually and makes all kinds of video. He then invites two more buddies to join in. Paula is still unconscious and has no clue that the drink she took was spiked and took control of her. (Most girls have no clue that someone is watching them in the club and ready to make a move to destroy their lives) This happened to a school teacher.

Paula wakes up the next morning: what am I doing here. Nick is nowhere around.

Paula discovers that she had sex last but not consensual.

She realizes that she was just set up and been raped (date rape).

Paula calls Ann Marie her best friend.

REVERSE THE TIDE

Ann Marie arrives two blocks from Nicks place

Paul: I think I been raped last night

Ann Marie: Do you know who it is you should report it to the police now and go get examined now.

Paula: What is Randy (my husband) going to think of me? He told me not to go out. Not to get up with girls out at night. Just take me to the hospital but please don't tell anyone.

Weeks later: she finds out that she is pregnant and its not Randy's. Now Paula seeks to get a private abortion; meanwhile Randy knows something is up.

HELD HOSTAGE IN IRAQ

Mark Denton: My brother is taken hostage in Iraq and there is this big thing on the news station. Carl Brown: Sorry to here that man

WORSHIP AT CHURCH FOR HEALING! (CHURCH SERVICE)

Pastor Bruce Steele - Church today's sermon is on the Woman at the well. "If you knew the Gift" This woman was married, found herself needing a man to fill the void places in her life. She found herself in need of a new husband. So she went through a few men that made her feel special a few more times. But in the midst of all of these relationships, she was still empty. However, God has a way of showing up. This woman ended up finding the most important companion ever in her life. She met Jesus Christ at the well. The one who name is above all names. She really did not recognize or know him until he told her that if she knew who he was that he would give her living water. Somehow that got into her spirit and she had to go and tell somebody. Jesus never judged her past relationships. He just wanted to her to start a new one with him. This woman at the well found the perfect man for her life. When she really understood that, she could not help herself. She had to tell every about someone that she met at the well. Have you ever had those kinds of chills to come over you when you knew the truth was starring you in the face with love? If you knew the gift, you would change your ways. If you knew the gift, your worship life would be for God. If you knew the gift, you would love people with genuine love, you would love God with all your heart, mind, soul and strength. Jesus is the gift given to men. It is time for you to meet Jesus and stop living for the world and other people to give you happiness. Jesus the one who was raised from the dead already gave you a joy that overflows in life, a peace that surpass understanding. He holds the key to you future and everlasting life. His arms are open for those who cry out and those that need mercy, for those who desire a relationship with him. Repent of your sin and ask Jesus to come into your heart. .

The Church and congregation people – Amen Pastor. Thank you Jesus for not judging me.

Choir Sings; upbeat song. Then a touching solo No weapon formed against me. Then Lord, take my hand. Take me to the Kings is a good song. Let sing that one next

Janelle is having flash back of Reggie raping her and walking out bragging with and zipping his pants. She keeps hearing, well you got what you asked for little girl! Girl shut up, nobody going to believe your behind

Alter Call: Reggie's family comes up. Michael family comes up before the altar. 100 people come up to receive Jesus Christ as Lord and Savoir. An altercation occurs between to brothers. Five deacons come between fast and pull both outside. Pastor continues with alter call. Prayer begins. Father we come before you with thanksgiving in the midst of trouble. In the midst of troubled hearts, you remind us that The enemy comes to kill, still and destroy. We come to give you glory Lord. We know the enemy comes to seek who he may devour. He comes in like a thief at night. He comes in the life of God's people to destroy families and friends.

Church is over: Michael and his mother meets Pastor at the door and Pastor tells Michael to keep trusting in God. The Lord will take you and this family forward in the blessings of the Lord. Honor him.

Bibliography

Dobson E.G., Feinberg, C.L., Hindson, E.E. Kroll, W. M., & Willmington H.L., (1994).Parallel Bible Commentary. *The complete King James Verson*, p 2438.

.

www.ingramcontent.com/pod-product-compliance
Lightning Source LLC
Chambersburg PA
CBHW071424090426
42737CB00011B/1563